OUR LAND REVENUE POLICY

IN

NORTHERN INDIA

OUR LAND REVENUE POLICY

IN

NORTHERN INDIA.

BY

CHARLES JAMES CONNELL

GYAN

Published by

GYAN

Gyan Publishing House
5, Ansari Road
Daryaganj, New Delhi-110002
Phone: 011-47034999, 9811692060
E-mail: books@gyanbooks.com

Distribution Network
gyanbooks.com
India, USA, Canada, UK, Australia, France

ISBN: 978-81-212-7352-7 (PB)
First Published, 1876

2nd Impression 2023

Printed at: Gyan Press, Delhi.

OUR LAND REVENUE POLICY IN NORTHERN INDIA
Author: CHARLES JAMES CONNELL

OUR LAND REVENUE POLICY

IN

NORTHERN INDIA.

BY

CHARLES JAMES CONNELL,

BENGAL CIVIL SERVICE.

CALCUTTA:

THACKER, SPINK AND CO.

BOMBAY: THACKER, VINING & CO. MADRAS: HIGGINBOTHAM & CO.

LONDON: W. THACKER & CO.

1876.

PREFACE.

THE main portion of this volume consists in the reproduction of a pamphlet, which was written in August 1874, and printed for private circulation among friends. Some of those to whom the pamphlet was sent were kind enough to say, that some passages and suggestions merited a larger audience; and, with considerable diffidence as to the value of its contents, I publish this attempt to present an untechnical description of the Native and the English revenue systems, and to offer some few proposals for the reform of our method of revenue-administration.

It was not possible to point out the defects in our present system without proving my assertions by frequent quotations from published official reports. It may be thought, that some few remarks or quotations have a savour of personality, and that allusions to the performances of fellow-officials, all of them my superiors in experience and in ability, betoken a want of good taste and decorum on the part of the writer.

I can only say, that nothing could be further from my thoughts or wishes than in any way to cast reflections upon any particular official, nor would it be possible to do so without great impropriety. It must be recollected, that the point which the writer would strive to impress upon the readers of this work is—not that the Settlement Officers or Collectors voluntarily fail in the performance of their difficult and onerous duties, but that our system, defective in its idea, and unsuitable in its form, urgently requires extensive reforms. It is impossible for officials, whether of ordinary or extraordinary ability, to carry out in any perfection a method of assessment which would probably tax beyond their powers the most highly-trained land-surveyors, and it is not reasonable to require, or expect a Collector, unaided by any adequate staff, and over-burdened with an immense variety of other duties, to perform the functions of an efficient revenue-administrator.

If a young officer may be allowed to say so without raising a smile, there is no one more impressed than I am with the extreme difficulty of securing a really fair assessment of the land-tax under our existing system, or more astonished at the indefatigable energy with which, in defiance of the limited duration of a day, the Collectors contrive to drive along the official omnibus with so few serious break-downs.

It is in the hope that this endeavour, insufficient and incomplete as it is, to explain the defects of the present system of collection and assessment of the land-tax, and to suggest a few remedial measures, may afford some aid to those earnest Indian officials, who realize the necessity for reform, that I offer these pages to the criticism of the Anglo-Indian public.

Want of leisure must be my apology for a perfunctory revision of the proof-sheets, and for the lengthy list of errata, as well as for the absence of an index.

TABLE OF CONTENTS.

PART I.

CHAPTER I.

THE LAND REVENUE ADMINISTRATION UNDER NATIVE GOVERNMENTS.

CHAPTER II.

OUR MODE OF ASSESSMENT OF THE LAND REVENUE.

CHAPTER III.

OUR SYSTEM OF COLLECTION OF THE LAND-TAX, AND THE DEFECTS IN OUR ADMINISTRATION.

PART II.

CHAPTER IV.

CHANGES REQUIRED IN OUR SYSTEM OF ASSESSMENT.

CHAPTER V.

PROPOSED CHANGES IN OUR SYSTEM OF COLLECTION OF THE LAND-TAX, AND IN OUR REVENUE ADMINISTRATION.

APPENDIX.

ERRATA.

Page	37,	line	21,	for 'unwillingly' read 'unwittingly.'
„	39,	„	13,	for 'possiblity' read 'possibility.'
„	46,	„	1,	omit 'understood.'
„	49,	„	7,	after 'just' read 'to take.'
„	51,	„	16,	omit inverted commas before 'all over.'
„	56,	„	29,	for 'minu' read 'minus.'
„	63,	„	27,	after 'waste' insert a comma.
„	67,	„	5,	after 'waste' read 'is.'
„	69,	„	23,	for 'deprecated' read 'depreciated.'
„	92,	„	18,	comma should be after 'that.'
„	96,	„	4,	for 'rents' read 'rent.'
„	103,	„	18,	after 'club' read 'too freely.'
„	112,	„	19,	for 'Davis' read 'Davies.'
„	117,	„	1,	for 'to be tilled' read 'to lie untilled.'
„	118,	„	10,	for 'apparently sound' read 'a most unsound.'
„	123,	„	21,	omit 'is.'
„	142,	„	23,	omit 'not.'
„	153,	„	4,	for 'tail' read 'tale.'
„	160,	„	3,	for 'on' read 'in.'
„	174, omit 'that' at the end of last line but one.			
„	176,	line	11,	omit comma after 'Talukdars.'
„	180,	„	8,	for 'government' read 'Governments.'
„	184,	„	22,	omit comma after 'impracticable.'
„	189,	„	19,	omit comma after 'misapprehension.'
„	193,	„	6,	after 'cannot' read 'successfully.'
„	198,	„	29,	for 'bestow' read 'bestows.'

OUR LAND REVENUE POLICY

IN

NORTHERN INDIA.

CHAPTER I.

THE LAND REVENUE ADMINISTRATION UNDER NATIVE GOVERNMENTS.

"The simple plan,
That they should take, who have the power,
And they should keep, who can."

DURING the last two or three years public attention has, in every province of Upper India, been prominently directed to this important subject. It is not an exaggeration to allege that, in almost every district of the North-West Provinces, of Oudh, of the Central Provinces, and of the Punjab, landed property is passing from the possession of the hereditary owners into the hand of strangers; the defects of the revenue system and of the revenue regulations have been admitted in three out of four provinces by the passing of Land Revenue Acts for the North-West Provinces and for the Punjab, while a similar measure has been proposed for Oudh.*

The intimate connection between the condition of the landed classes and our revenue policy needs no illustration. It is manifest that the prosperity of the proprietors of land mainly depends upon our principle of revenue assessment and on our system of revenue collection; it is not too much to say that on the proper exercise of the powers entrusted to Settlement Officers and Collectors hangs the future welfare of all owners of land, from the possessor of

* The Chief Commissioner of the Central Provinces also, as will be seen from p. 24, has addressed the Government of India on this question.

half a county to the co-sharer whose portion in the estate of a large proprietary community is represented by a dozen acres of rice land. No less interested is the humble tiller of the soil, whose bread depends upon the lightness or severity with which the assessor taxes his landlord's property.*

Many scattered attempts have been made to account for the very general indigence of the landed classes of Upper India, and from time to time in various papers and periodicals there have appeared disjointed and fragmentary onslaughts on our principles of revenue assessment; many conflicting theories have been started, but no one writer has as yet undertaken to gather up all the tangled skeins into one thread, and to present a connected account of the causes which have led to these extensive and continuous transfers of landed property, and of the manner in which our assessment and collection of the land-tax injuriously affect the interests both of the landowners and of the cultivators.

An endeavour will be made in the following pages to set forth the extent to which Government action and Government interference may fairly be held responsible for the disastrous result, and in what degree the calamity, so

* "I believe that the happiness of the bulk of the inhabitants of the Western Provinces depends more on revenue settlements than on any other thing whatever." (Sir C. Metcalfe's minute, dated 7th November 1830.) Yet so little does this seem to be understood, that Colonel Chesney, in his work on "Indian Polity," dismisses the land-tax in two pages; and Mr. Elliott, in his book entitled "Concerning John's Indian Affairs," has only one reform to propose in regard to our land-revenue administration (*viz.*, that the Revenue Boards should be abolished, and that Secretaries should be substituted for them to act between the Collectors and the Government), although his proposals number in all twenty-four remedial measures. If I recollect aright, General Marriott, in a public lecture not long ago delivered in London, pointed to an increased land-tax as the best mode of placing the Indian finances on a satisfactory footing; and Mr. Grant-Duff shows no sign in his Notes published in the Contemporary Review that he has any but a very roseate view of the excellencies of our revenue administration.

far as it affects the proprietors of estates, is due to the incapacity of the landholding classes themselves; finally, a few practicable remedies are proposed in the belief that they would considerably lessen, if they might not altogether remove, some of the causes which are fast driving the old proprietors from their ancestral estates.

It is necessary, however, for a right understanding of the condition of the landed classes and cultivators under our rule, that some description should be given of the revenue system of our predecessors; the two methods can then be readily compared, and it will then be easier to consider whether any portion of the native procedure might not be beneficially imitated by the present rulers of this country; we shall also realize with greater certainty the position of the owners of land under the former system of administration.

At this distance of time it is difficult to find any good authority for a picture of the native revenue system as it obtained in the North-West Provinces before their annexation. The Province of Oudh, however, was only incorporated in 1856 A.D., and not only are such works as Sir W. Sleeman's Tour in Oudh accessible for consultation, but those who are now stationed in that province have many opportunities of hearing from eye-witnesses how the government of that kingdom was conducted prior to its seizure by us just before the mutiny.*

The land in Oudh belonged mainly to the strong Rajput clans, who, many generations ago, after their expulsion by the Mahomedans from their old territories in the north, marched southwards, under the leadership of the Rajahs or heads of their race, and conquered the country from

* This description of the Oudh revenue system will apply generally to those Oudh districts which were ceded to the English Government by Sáadat Ali Khan in 1801 A.D., and which now form part of the North-West Provinces, *viz.*, Rohilkund, Allahabad, Furruckabad, Cawnpore, Mainpuri, Etawah, Gorakpur, Azimgarh, and Fatehpur.

the Bhars, Doms, or other early landowners and settlers; these tribes have since been left for the most part in undisturbed proprietorship of their estates, subject to the due payment of the Government land-tax. In various parts of the country there were also many villages which belonged to members of scattered and broken clans, to Mahomedan conquerors and settlers, to successful soldiers and courtiers who had received grants from the Delhi Emperor, or the Oudh Nawabs, to Brahman communities, the family priests of the Rajput clans, to the kanungo families of Kayaths, and in a few cases to members of low castes, as Kurmis, Ahirs, and Lodhs.*

---

* I take as an instance the history of pargana Mohsna in the Lucknow district. It appears that about the 14th century this part of the country was held under the sway of two Kurmi chiefs; Rae Damar ruled at Raepore, and Rae Dhandu at Kathwara, and the story goes that these Kurmis had supplanted the Bhars and other aboriginal inhabitants.

The Kurmis refused or neglected to pay their revenue to the Delhi monarchs, and the tradition is that the Paonwar and Chauhan clans were despatched to subdue and dispossess them.

The Paonwars were led by two brothers, Rae Deo Ridh Rae and Ram Singh, the sons of Rajah Radisar of Deogarh; the Chauhans marched in two bands, one under the captaincy of two brothers, Acharaj and Bacheraj, and the others fought under Kesari Sing, an alleged cadet of the Chauhans of Mainpuri.

The Kurmis were conquered, and their villages were seized by the victorious Rajputs. The Chauhans obtained, or have since colonized, fifty-two villages; and the Paonwars acquired the remainder with the exception of a village granted to some warlike retainers of Rae Deo, and a small property granted to some Kayaths, or members of the writer caste, who accompanied the Paonwars in their expedition as their accountants and lawyers.

Rae Deo, as the head of the clan, received the largest share, and Ram Sing a smaller estate. When Rae Deo died his property was divided between his three sons by the family lawyer, the kanungo Tilok Chand. The headship of the clan remained in the family of the eldest son, Dugur Deo; and he is the ancestor of the present talukdar.

At the time of the conquest, the Rajah or chief of the clan received the largest share of the clan domains, and his descendants have since held as the hereditary owners; the cadets of the house settled in the surrounding and outlying villages; and the Rajah's mud fort, built in the centre of the clan estate, and carefully surrounded with jungle and bamboo hedges, formed the stronghold of defence for the whole proprietary body in case of attacks from neighbours or Government officials.

In the time of Sáadat Ali Khan, the wisest ruler that Oudh has ever posssessed, the land-tax was annually fixed by Government officials under the direct superintendence of the Nawab, and special officers were appointed to collect the assessed demand from each district of the province. His successors, however, who were in general corrupt and effete rulers, compelled to contribute a large subsidy to the British Government, and utterly incompetent both in talents and in disposition to conduct public business, abandoned the system of direct assessment and collection, and farmed out the revenue of the different districts to the highest bidder.

As is notorious, misrule in Oudh gradually increased in intensity, until it wàs deemed necessary in 1856 A.D. to annex the kingdom. The clans with the aid of their chiefs* had, as in Gonda, Hardui, Unao, Partabgarh, Luck-

---

The various cadets of the house received different villages as their share of the paternal domains, but at the present time the Rajah holds fifty-one villages, and the descendant of the second son of Rae Deo has twenty-three villages; the Chauhans still possess all their old domains. (Lucknow Settlement Report.)

* These chiefs have been confounded indiscriminately with the other talukdars and with the zamindars of Lower Bengal. Sir C. Wingfield found occasion to correct this misapprehension in 1865; yet writers like Dr. Thornton (Indian Public Works, 1875) still choose to class them all under one head, and to quote Man Singh's rise to eminence as an example of the origin of all the large landowners in Oudh (p. 235). Those who know Oudh will read about the "new fangled Oudh Aristocracy" with intense amusement. "The great majority

now, and Rai Bareli, maintained a successful fight against the Government officials and the jungle robbers; but in many instances the villages of small landowners, who were too weak and disunited to protect their properties, were incorporated, either with or without their consent, in the estates of these powerful heads of clans, or were seized by one or other of the Government revenue-farmers in payment of arrears of revenue.

There can be little doubt, however, that the native revenue system,* so far as it was carried out without excessive violence and oppression,—that is, the system itself,—was eminently adapted to the conditions of life in this country and to the character of the people. The revenue demand was roughly fixed each year shortly before the autumn harvest, and written engagements were then taken for the payment of the assessment, but a revision of the tax was made when the prospects of the spring harvest were ascertained, and, according to the prospects of the crops as detailed by the kanungos, the demand was raised, lowered, or maintained at the original level.†

---

of the Hindoo talukdars of Oudh are the heads of houses whose ancestors acquired their possessions by colonization and conquest between the years 1200 and 1300 A.D. The first settlers were fugitives from the Mahomedan invasion of Upper India, and from them descend all the great families in Eastern Oudh. Each clan was under a head, in whom all proprietorship and authority were vested, but the clans became divided into houses, the heads of which are the present talukdars. There was much subdivision among the younger branches, and village communities were thus formed." (P. 16, Oudh Blue Book on Tenant Right, 1867 Letter of Chief Commissioner to Government of India.)

* Reference is made more especially to the system of direct assessment by Government officers as maintained by Sáadut Ali Khan.

† Cf. pp. 7, 8, 9, Notes on Tenant Right, &c. N. W. P. Government Press, 1869:—

"Where village proprietorship prevailed the rents were collected by the proprietor, and he was responsible for the entire sum to the Government. For special reasons he might be set aside, and the rent collected by a Government nominee. In either case

If the landowner refused to accept the engagement, the village was either farmed or held direct; the proprietors retained all their seer (*i.e.*, all the land tilled by themselves with their own ploughs and farm servants) at favorable rates, and sometimes received also nankar or a cash allowance, usually in the shape of a deduction from the rent due for their seer fields. When the landowners accepted the engagements, they had to give sureties for punctual payment, and these sureties were generally the local chaudhris, the kanungos,* influential bankers, or the larger landowners of the neighbourhood; if the landowners failed to pay, their sureties paid up, seized the defaulters, and imprisoned them till they raised the sum; if the surety could not succeed in arresting the defaulters, he took possession of the

---

the proprietor was entitled to hold a portion of the estate rent-free, or at a privileged rent, as recognition of his proprietorship. Such land was called *nankar*, *seer*, or *malikana*. For the convenience and security of Government, it was customary, instead of making the proprietor render an account of the rent, to estimate the sum of them, and after deducting his privileged holding, to take an engagement (kabuliat) from him for the amount. The transaction then assumed the form of a lease; the proprietor was responsible for the sum specified; if his rents fell below it, he was the loser by so much; if they exceeded, he was the gainer,—but not always very secure of his gain under Governments that were no respecter of contracts. The lease was made ordinarily at the beginning of the agricultural season, but was often subject to revision towards its close. The amount of privileged land called 'nankar,' 'malikana,' &c., was not fixed at any invariable proportion of the estate. Throughout the North-West, however, it is very generally held that the proprietor was, under an ancient custom, entitled to receive a proportion equal to one-tenth of the area of assets."

* The kanungos were the hereditary registrars of landed property; there was at last one for each pargana; in fact they were originally the lawyers of the country families, and, in addition to these duties, they had to keep the official records of land revenue assessment and collection for the information of the Government revenue-collectors and farmers. They usually owned a small estate in their pargana, and they were persons of considerable influence under the native administration; all deeds of mortgage or sale were sealed by them and registered in their office.

estate and collected the rents. If there were no sureties, or, if it was thought desirable to punish the refractory landowners, the Government revenue farmer sent off the nearest commandant of troops with full powers to collect the rents and to apply them to the payment of his men; the latter marched off to the village with his soldiers, drove off the landowners to the jungles,* collected what he could from the cultivators; if he was resisted, he burnt the houses and carried off all the bullocks and other moveable property as spoil; next year the village would probably be well-nigh deserted; the owners would be hiding in the jungles; the cultivators, being without seed or cattle, would be

* Sir William Sleeman notes (p. 286, Vol. II) that there were in Oudh in 1849-50 twenty-four belts of jungle, covering a space of 886 square miles at a rough computation. "In the jungles the landholders found shooting, fishing, and security for themselves and families; grazing ground for their horses and cattle, and fuel and grass for their followers; and they can hardly understand how landholders of the same rank in other countries can continue to exist without them." Besides these large forest tracts, there were smaller bush-grown plots of waste land in the neighbourhood of most villages, affording shelter to fugitive landlords and tenants. The effects of misrule soon disappeared in Oudh. "If a landholder took to rebellion and plunder, he is followed by all his retainers and clansmen, and their families; and the cultivators of other classes, feeling no longer secure, go and till lands in other estates till they are invited back. The cowherds and shepherds, who live by the produce of their cattle and sheep, remain and thrive by the abundance of pasture lands from which the rich spring and harvest crops have disappeared. These cattle and sheep graze on them and enrich the soil by restoring to it a portion of those elements of fertility of which a long succession of harvests has robbed it. The landholder and his followers in the meantime subsist and enrich themselves by the indiscriminate plunder of the surrounding country, and are at last invited back by a weak and wearied Government to re-occupy their lands, improved by this salutary fallow, at a lower rate of rent, or no rent at all for some years, and a remission of all balances for past years on account of *paemalee*, or treading down of crops during the disorder which has prevailed. The cultivators return to occupy their old lands so enriched at a reduced rate of rent, and in two or three years these lands are, however, again carpeted with a beautiful variety of spring and autumn crops." (*Idem*, pp. 42, 43, Vol. II.)

unable to plough any of the fields; the revenue farmer's receipts would decrease, and the owners would be invited back with a promise of a reduced land-tax; the fields, having lain fallow in the interval, would yield an abundant crop, and in a short time the village would be as prosperous as ever.

The landowner would have received a warning to be more punctual in his payments, and the revenue farmer would have learnt the impolicy of a resort to excessive violence.

There were neither accumulating arrears of land-revenue, nor ruinous back debts, to weigh down the proprietors; there were no unsatisfied decrees of court to drive debtors to hopeless despair; they came back from their court of bankruptcy, the jungle forest, free from encumbrances; the land-tax was fixed with some regard to the prospects of the coming harvest; arrears were remitted when the impossibility of payment within the year was clearly demonstrated, but when the defaulting landowners were found with money, they were compelled to pay up the revenue demand in full; the proximity of the jungle, and the certainty of a serious diminution of income, checked the Government officials or the local farmers from using, as a rule, too much violence; villages or shares of village were indeed from time to time compulsorily sold or mortgaged, but in those days the wheel of fortune revolved quickly and suddenly; an estate acquired to-day by a forced sale, by voluntary transfer, or by downright violence, might be lost to-morrow; the new owner might be disgraced or killed, and the old owner would recover his ancestral estates.

There was no decree of court to stifle out for ever all hope of restoration; there were no deeds of sale upheld by a strong and permanent Government; there could be no black despair in those days of changeful misrule; much oppression, much crime, and much misgovernment there were undeniably, but it may be doubted whether the landowners would not prefer the chance of murder or pillage to the dead level of hopeless ruin, to which our system is fast reducing them.

It is a mistake to suppose that any exact regard was paid to the amount of rent actually collected by the landowners; the system of assessment was one of rough bargain; no rent-rolls of any kind were presented to the Government officials, or written out in the offices of the pargana kanungos; these latter officials merely maintained registers to show the annual demand from each estate for all past years; the village accountant was a private servant of the landowners, and his accounts were made out solely for the latter's inspection and information; the revenue farmer at the time of the fixation of the yearly demand in September was guided in his assessment by the detailed statements of past taxation, and by the reports of the officials in respect to the means of the landowners and the condition of their estates. Theoretically, the landowner was required to pay up in full the rents of the cultivators, with a deduction of a certain sum as a cash allowance; but in assuming the rental, the lands in his own cultivation were rated at a low rent; as a matter of fact, there were no means of ascertaining what the gross collections of the landowner might amount to; the past year's demand, which in theory represented that year's full rental minus the above deductions, was the only guide at hand for the determination of the revenue demand.*

---

* Sir W. Muir, on p. 8 of his note on sub-settlements, writes:—" It will be obvious that the distinction between rent and revenue created by our limitation of the Government demand had no existence under the native rule: rent and revenue were convertible terms. The drawback allowed to the proprietor was given, not, as with us, in the shape of a ratable deduction from the estimated rental, but by the assignment of land which was subtracted from the rent-roll. This, with the perquisites of management, manorial receipts, and the benefit from those hidden sources which the officers of Government were unable

It is easy to understand, therefore, that while in many cases a very oppressive land-tax was assessed on the estates of the smaller and less powerful landowners, those who were of any consideration frequently escaped with a very light demand; in all cases the landowner might entertain a hope that by bribing the subordinate officials, by assuming a bold tone of defiance, or by deceiving the revenue farmer and his subordinates as to his wealth, or the prosperity of his villages, he might be able to obtain the reduction of his land-tax, or at least prevent its enhancement. Even if he failed in September, and his estate was heavily assessed, he might make a more successful attempt after the harvesting of the autumn crop; at the worst he could abscond and wait for better times, or he could curry favor with the revenue farmers, and at the end of the year obtain a remission of the balances due.

A good description is given by Sir W. Sleeman of this kind of revenue administration. A village (Poknapur) was the property of some Brahmans, and, according to tradition, it had descended from father to son for fifty-two generations; the revenue official suddenly raised the demand from Rs. 400

---

to explore (in other words, embezzlement from the rental), formed the only sources of proprietary income."

This account would be quite correct if Sir W. Muir had only inserted the words "*in theory*" before "no existence," for *in fact* no attempt was made to prepare an accurate estimate of the existing rents of an estate, and the Government officials never sought to interfere between the proprietors and their cultivators by fixing rents to be paid by the tenants. Again, *in theory*, the landowner only received a nankar allowance of ten per cent. on the estimated rental; but *in practice* he obtained any sum which he could succeed by threats, bribes, or haggling in inducing the Government officers to allow.

It is not probable that the system of yearly assessments checked cultivation or prevented improvement; the landowners could always hope to make a good bargain, and where there was no fear of violence, they kept their villages well tilled; as to improvements, neither our assessments, whether permanent or for 30 years, nor the native system, has seduced landowners into spending capital on wells, drainage, or improved methods of husbandry.

to Rs. 450; the Brahmans stoutly refused to pay this increase; then the revenue farmer offered the lease to a neighbouring large proprietor named Hindu Sing; the Brahmans declined to pay the latter; he at once despatched a body of his retainers, who plundered and burnt the village, and killed some of the Brahmans. The Lucknow Government took umbrage at these proceedings of Hindu Sing, and he was obliged to abscond over the border to one of our districts. The revenue farmer seeing, that, unless he pacified the Brahmans, he would gain no receipts at all from the property, replaced the old landowners in possession of their village, and reduced their land-tax to Rs. 250; soon afterwards it was again raised to Rs. 400, but some robbers attacked and plundered the village, and the Brahmans again succeeded in obtaining a reduction to Rs. 250.* We read that a landowner named Loni Sing, of Mithauli, paid to the king's treasury a tax of Rs. 50,000 only, although his rents were supposed to amount to Rs. 1,50,000, and it is remarked that " he is considered one of his best subjects."†

* Again the Resident gives an account of the estate held by the Ahbans clan; the head of the clan, Mahomed Hasan Khan, who had been converted to Mahomedanism, resided in his fort of Jalalpur; this fort was concealed from view, and protected by a bamboo fence; he had twelve villages revenue-free as nankar, and he paid revenue for the remainder according to the roughly calculated estimate of his rent-roll.

† I have not given all the details of this system, since it will be necessary to use several vernacular terms which may confuse, or at any rate weary, the ordinary reader; in this note, therefore, I give a full and detailed account of the " ijara" system as carried out in Oudh shortly before annexation.

The chakladar or revenue farmer of a circle (chakla) was appointed at the beginning of the Fasli year; he gave in a petition to the Wazir, and the candidate who offered the largest sum, and gave the best security, as a rule obtained the appointment; he was presented with a khillat, and arrangements were then made with him in regard to the forces which he was to maintain, and the instalments in which he was to pay the revenue; generally he was directed to pay the sum agreed upon in ten instalments, called kists.

Mention is made of the estate of a landowner named Sheobaksh, whose rental was assumed to amount to

---

On the arrival of the chakladar on the borders of the district which he had obtained in farm, he was received by the subordinate revenue officials, and on his arrival at the kutcherry, or head office, he appointed the "peshkar," or dewan, the "wasil-baki-navis," or clerk of accounts, for the collections and balances of the revenue, the "jama-kharch-navis," or clerk of disbursements, the "itlak-navis," or clerk of processes, and the "potdar," or treasurer; the latter was usually the agent of the banker who had given security for the chakladar; he also appointed a tahsildar or deputy collector for each parganah or sub-division of the district. He then examined the office registers, which showed the jamas of past year (hakikat jama), the number of the kists, and the character of the zamindars (dasturulam), the names of the various villages, the lists of those landowners who would attend his office when summoned, and of those who could and would give security for the payment of their jamas, the nankar or cash allowances made to different landowners, and the lists of all solvent and reliable sureties.

The landowners were summoned, and on their appearance they offered presents, and arrangement was then made for the assessment of their villages; about ten kists were fixed for the payment of the fixed land-tax. If any landholder did not appear, a fresh summons was issued, and this time probably a sowar or horseman would be sent with it; the fee would be Re. 1-4 a day, besides the sowar's food, and of all such receipts the chakladar received two-thirds, while the process-server got one-third; if the landowner was under the protection of any official, he was summoned through the surety; if the landowner still refused to attend, forces were sent out to arrest him, or, if he required it, surety for his good treatment was given; in August and September the revenue was finally settled, and if the landholder refused to sign the kabuliat (or agreement to pay), he was either put into the havalat (prison), or his village was farmed to some neighbour, and he was allowed to return home; if he accepted, security was required from him, unless he could be relied on as a punctual payer of his revenue; if all means failed, a kabz (or contract) was given to a commandant of troops, who either agreed to go to the village, collect and pay in a stipulated sum, he being responsible for any failure to collect, or else he signed a receipt for a certain sum, representing perhaps the pay of his troops, and he was then allowed to go and collect what he could, and no account of his collections was required on his return. When the landowner signed the kabuliat, he received in return a patta

Rs. 54,640. He was called on to pay a land-tax of Rs. 37,053; he resolutely declined to pay, and shut himself up in his mud fort, where the Government officials dared not attack him.

The State did not, as a rule, manage to collect any sum approaching to half assets from the larger landowners; in one place it is stated that a large landowner was required to pay Rs. 1,88,000 out of an assumed rent-roll of Rs. 2,56,000, but that, as a fact, his rental was much greater than, and perhaps double, this sum.

Sir W. Sleeman describes the estates of the heads of the Janwars of Kheri; how each Rajah had a fort

---

(lease), showing the amount of his jama, the kists, and the allowed cash deduction for the different villages. The tahsildar appointed Shahnas or watchmen with orders to see that the crops were not carried off, in all cases where the landowner's behaviour could not be relied on.

If the jama was so heavy that no arrangement could be made, the landowner, if in custody, asked for a jamog; the chakladar then sent an official to the village, and the latter proceeded to the village with the landowner; the tenants were summoned, and they were ordered to enter into an agreement with the jamogdar to pay their rents direct to him. These (as Sleeman notes, p. 203, Vol. I) might be the whole, or less than the whole, of the amount due to Government by the landowner; if the tenants failed to pay the rents in full, the landholder was bound to make up the deficiencies; at the end of the year he also bound himself to make good whatever might be due over and above the sum which the tenants might agree to pay to the jamogdar. This process was termed "jamog lagana," or the transference of responsibility from the landholder to the tenant; the salary of the jamogdar was paid by the landowners, who distributed the sum due by a percentage added to the rents of each tenant; the tenants bound themselves by written engagements not to pay any of their rents to the landowners. Sometimes, if the landowners or tenants were proved to be desperate characters, the nearest commandant of troops was appointed jamogdar. At the end of the revenue year the accounts were made up, and when it was shown that there was a balance due from any estate, the landowner was either called on to pay in all the arrears by a sale or mortgage of his property, or the estate was held kham as a punishment; under any circumstance, the balance was finally struck off either as charhna (*i.e.*, remission), or as incapable of realization, before arrangements were made for the coming year.

surrounded by a strong fence of bamboos, and mounted with good guns; and how it was impossible to collect even a moderate land-tax, although the lands in their estates were well tilled, and were yielding abundant rent to the owners; the profits were spent in the maintenance of large bands of armed retainers, but the cultivators and sub-holders were treated with kindness, and protected against all violence.

The clans of Bangarman contrived to maintain their position in the worst days of native misrule;* the landholders throughout the neighbourhood were leagued together for mutual defence against the exactions of the revenue collectors and farmers. On hearing the concerted signal, which was generally the firing of a matchlock, all the clansmen were bound to take up arms, and hurry to the assistance of their attacked neighbours; an offensive and defensive league, in fact, extended through the length and breadth of that part of the country; the revenue officers were powerless to pillage the landowners, and the villages were all thickly populated and richly cultivated; the land-tax therefore was fixed with moderation, and collected without violence, for "the landholders were solemnly pledged to aid each other to the death when oppressed or attacked by the Government officials." One Nazim was reported to have reduced the tax by Rs. 40,000, in order to induce the landholders to pay up the revenue demanded and to abstain from acts of violence.

---

* The Unao settlement officer records—"By far the greater portion of the district being held by independent proprietary communities, descendants of the original colonizers, who drove out and exterminated the aborigines, notwithstanding the anarchy which prevailed for so many years previous to annexation, they have to a great extent held their own to the last, and though often deprived of the direct engagement of their village by outsiders, favorites of the men in power, in the end always succeeded in re-establishing themselves and recovering possession." (Pp. 62,63, Settlement Report.)

Cf. Sleeman's "Oudh," Vol. II, pp. 11, 12, 15.

If, as in these parts of Oudh, the small independent landowners contrived to maintain possession of their estates in spite of the oppressive exactions of the revenue farmers, still more secure and comfortable was the position of the under-proprietor, who held his village in sub-infeudation to the large landholders of the trans-Ghagra districts of the province.*

Allusion is not made here to those whose villages, once held in independent proprietorship, had been forcibly, or at their own desire, included in the estate of one of the powerful northern Rajahs, but to those who had purchased rights from the latter, and who held their lands as sub-proprietors on payment of the sums annually demanded in the shape of rent by their lords.

It was a constant practice of these Rajahs to sell what was called a "birt" right to resident cultivators. When they were embarrassed to pay the Government revenue, when they had been defeated in a fight with the Government

---

* Mr. W. C. Benett, C.S., in his report on the Rai Bareli clans, gives a good picture of the position and character of the Hindu chiefs:— "Nor were the talukdars without a useful purpose. Ignorant, proud, cruel, and stained by every meanness and every crime, the district (Rai Bareli) has much reason to be thankful to them. In the midst of the anarchy of royal oppression, they were the only elements of law and order. Their power resisted the tyranny from without, and prevented the utter destruction of industry and wealth, while within their own manors their feudal courts administered a rude and serviceable justice. Politically they had a still deeper significance; the chieftains and the retainers were the only units of Hindu society susceptible of development, and redeemed the country from the dead level of dowerless slaves under an all-powerful Sultan. Nor were signs wanting that the throne was soon to fall before the rising national life. The central executive was already paralyzed, while the ties of family and clan were being widened, and consolidated on a territorial basis. Had we stayed our hand, it is possible that even now a Hindu Raja might be ruling a Hindu nation from the ancient seat of Hindu religion and empire on a throne supported by an aristocracy lately developed from the hierarchy of chieftains whose ancient ranks had been reinforced by the addition of all that was most vigorous by the late regimé." (Pp. 64, 65.)

officials, when they stood in need of a sum of ready-money to celebrate the marriage of their daughters with fitting pomp, when they desired to attract cultivators to cut down a jungle and plough up waste, or when they wished to induce old residents to remain in the village, if it was exposed to the attacks of robbers or to the raids of their neighbours, they would for a certain sum grant to a Brahman Thakur or other cultivator a deed (birt patr) under which the grantee became entitled to one of two privileges:—either the right to hold a lease of the village with a deduction of one-tenth of the stipulated rental, generally calculated on the supposed assets of the property at the time of the purchase,* or, if the Rajah should in any year refuse to grant him the lease, or should require too high a sum, the right to receive one-tenth of the gross rental in cash or in grain. The one-tenth would generally signify the holding of his own land at merely nominal rents; in some estates one-fourth was the allowance; the custom varied in different localities and in different estates.

* The allowance of one-tenth is apparently copied from the one-tenth theoretically deducted from the assumed rental of independently held estates in the shape of nankar or seer, at the time of the fixation of the land-tax by the Government officials.

In the Balrampur pargana the custom was different. The birtia received the one-tenth cash deduction, in the years when he had the lease of the village; in other years he held a small portion of the village area rent-free; this land was called "dih," and it was formally set apart by the Rajah's agent at the time of the execution of the birt patr.

In other parganas the birtia received seer, *i.e.*, held land at low rates or rent-free, when he lost the lease; but in such cases the grant of seer was specially made; he had no right to hold land at low rates in the absence of a special contract, commuting the payment of one-tenth of the gross produce by the allowance of land.

In 1826 the Collector of Gorakpur made a report concerning the birtias of that district. The Board of Revenue were doubtful as to the rights of these birtias, because their title-deeds did not refer to the payment of any purchase-money; in many estates, however, the Hindu chief was too careful in regard to his reputation (izzat), to allow it to be publicly stated, or recorded, that he had *sold* any under-proprietary right to his tenants.

Just as there was no rent-roll for the information of the Government revenue collectors, so there was no rent-roll filed by the "birtia" for the inspection of his superior; the question of payment was decided therefore in a rough-and-ready way on the basis of compromise, and the birtia's actual receipts would considerably exceed the nominal nine-tenths of the rack-rent of the total cultivated area. The Rajah of course protected his sub-holders from the Government officials, and, as he had no desire to drive them away to a neighbouring estate or into the jungles, he treated them himself with a certain consideration; the birtias could sell or mortgage their rights, as they pleased, subject to his confirmation, which he signified by affixing his sign-manual on the deed of sale or mortgage. So extensively did this sub-infeudation prevail that, in the estate of the Rajah of Bamnipur in Gonda, there is scarcely a village which is not held by these birtias; similarly in the Burhapara pargana (revenue subdivision) and in the Birwah estate most of the villages are held by these under-proprietors, and the estate of the Rajah of Mankapur was and is now in this condition.

The King of Oudh, in a letter dated 31st August 1823, tells the Resident "that the villages and estates of the large refractory talukdars were as flourishing and populous as they possibly can be, and there are many estates among them which yield more than two and three times the amount at which they have been assessed; and even if troops should be stationed there to prevent the cultivation of the land till the balances are liquidated, the talukdars immediately come forward and, in spite of everything, cultivate the lands of their estates, so that their profits from the land are even greater than those of the Government." Sir W. Sleeman adds that this picture is a very fair one, and as applicable to the state of Oudh during his tour (1850) as in 1823.*

* Sir W. Sleeman's (Vol. I, p. 57). It is amusing to read in Mr. Markham's report presented to Parliament, 1871-72, that "Akbar

No doubt a great number of villages were seized by force from the ancestral landowners by such men as Rajah Darshan Singh, and in a smaller degree by many of the wealthier and more powerful Rajahs, as those of Ekauna, Pyagpur, Bhinga, Chanda, Nanpara, and the Chehdwara Kalhans and others;* in many cases, however, the ancestral

---

recognized no proprietors, and the rent was the Government demand. We have created a body of proprietors in the N. W. P. with powers, which none but the Government ever claimed before, over the original occupants of the soil." Dr. Thornton appears to hold this view, but another official of the India Office, Sir J. W. Kaye, had a much truer conception of the real nature of land tenure. The Hindu chiefs have held their estates, and acted as the heads of their different clans, since 1300 A.D., yet it is declared in an official report that Akbar recognized no proprietors of land; similarly the Rajput village communities have retained undisturbed possession of their villages, and Todar Mal neither wished nor attempted to dispossess them. The land-settlement was made with the landholders on the basis of a calculation of the gross outturn of the total cultivated area of each village. As Mr. King wrote in his Partabgarh report—"for the last 600 or 800 years the landowning classes have been, broadly, the Rajput clans, now in the various parganas of this district." (P. 164, Partabgarh Settlement Report.)

* The Rajah of the Singha Chanda estate, for instance, did not, it is believed, possess a single village in the Gonda district prior to 1230F., and now in 1283F. he enjoys a property which comprises no less than 243 villages, and most of these villages were acquired on alleged deeds of sale or mortgage; his brother Ramdat Pande was a very influential and wealthy banker, and was the usual surety on behalf of the smaller landowners of the district for their due payment of the land-tax; many failed to pay at different times; they were then seized and imprisoned by the surety, and, to escape from confinement, they signed deeds of sale of their villages, in which the purchase-money was represented by the sum due to the banker on account of money paid by him to the revenue collector to clear off the balance of revenue owed by his clients. When the present Rajah became himself the revenue collector, he similarly extracted deeds of sale from the revenue defaulters. He is not a man of the same eminence as his brother, and very possibly the estate would have fallen to pieces, had not the annexation of Oudh taken place within six years of his brother's murder (1850 A.D.)

owners voluntarily placed themselves under the protection of their more powerful neighbours, in order to obtain immunity from the exactions of the Government farmers; the estate of Mohant Harcharn Dass was, for instance, formed entirely by voluntary transfers; his predecessor, Mohant Gur Narain Dass, was a well known and most respectable Lucknow resident, and his estate was never interfered with by the revenue collectors, since, in consideration of his high station, he was allowed to pay his revenue direct to the Lucknow treasury; many landowners therefore transferred their villages to him by fictitious deeds of sale or mortgage, in order to obtain his protection, and he allowed them to retain possession on payment of a small sum in excess of the Government land-tax.

In giving this account of the Oudh revenue system, it must not be understood that there is any desire to conceal or gloss over the frightful misrule which prevailed during the half century preceding annexation. The horrible details of the barbarities committed by such fiends in human shape as Raghoba Singh, the Nazim of Goudah-Bharaich, or by robbers like Ganga Buksh Sing and Bhuri Khem, as recounted by Sir William Sleeman,* were sufficient to amply justify, nay, to necessitate, the decided interference of the English Government. This account has been written to show that, in many respects, the Rajahs, their subholders, and many of the smaller independent proprietors were fairly well off under the rule of the King of Oudh, even on the face of terrible misgovernment.

Above all, although a great number of estates were transferred by sale and mortgage, still the great majority of landowners retained possession of their hereditary villages, while, as already remarked, even to the dispos-

* Among the commonest tortures appear to have been whipping naked women, rubbing gunpowder on men's beards, and then setting them on fire, cudgelling pregnant wives, trampling children to death, thrusting red-hot ramrods into the victim's body, and pulling out tongues with red-hot pincers. (Sir W. Sleeman's, Vol. I, p. 168.)

sessed landowner there was still left the anchor of hope, just as "Epimetheus when griefes and evils flew abroad, at last shut the lid and kept Hope in the bottom of the vessel;" the feeling of despair was not yet crushing out the hearts of the Oudh landowners; the misrule prevailing held men's hearts by hopes, when it could not by satisfaction, and "no evil appeared so peremptory, but that it had some outlet of hope." The evicted birtia or the ousted landowner found a secure refuge in the jungle forest, in which he could patiently wait for the turning of the tide, and ponder over the uses of adversity; let the worst come, he was seldom reduced to the desperate state of a rack-rented tenant-at-will; he had his sword and his shield, and, as long as those remained to him, he could fight, and at least strike a good blow for his ancestral fields.

So it is not surprising to find Sir William Sleeman recording that "the people generally, or at least a great part of them, would prefer to reside in Oudh, under all the risks to which these contests expose them, than in our own districts under the evils the people are exposed to from the uncertainties of our law, the multiplicity and formality of our courts, the pride and negligence of those who preside over them, and the corruption and insolence of those who must be employed to prosecute or defend a cause in them, and to enforce the fulfilment of a decree when passed."

He adds that "the members of the landed aristocracy of Oudh always speak with respect of the administration in our territories, but generally end with remarking on the cost and uncertainty of the law in civil cases, and the gradual decay under its operation of all the ancient families. A less and less proportion of the annual produce of their lands is left to them in our periodical settlements of the land revenue, while family pride makes them expend the same sums on the marriage of their children, in religious and other festivals, personal servants, and hereditary retainers. They fall into balance, incur heavy debts, and estate after estate is put up for auction, and the proprietors are reduced to poverty. They say that four times more of those families have gone to decay in the half of the territory made over to us in 1801, than in the half reserved by the Oudh sovereign; and this is, I fear, true. They named the families, but I cannot remember them."*

The district histories compiled by the Oudh settlement officers undoubtedly support these assertions. On examining, for example, the reports of the settlement of the Lucknow district, it appears that, prior to the re-assessment of the land-tax, the only parvenu landowners holding estates were the descendants of a former royal minister who had acquired six villages, and a banker who had secured a considerable property in Lucknow and Unao on alleged sales and mortgages; one large proprietor had increased his hereditary domains by seizing some villages belonging to his feebler neighbours, and an old Pathan freebooter had managed to leave his sons a property of some importance. All the other landholders had been long settled in the district; the Chauhans of Amosi retained all their old villages but two, and the Sheikhs of Nagram had held their lands uninterruptedly for twelve generations; the Bazad Khels had settled there seven generations ago; the ancestors of the Chauhans of Bhauli, who held their thirty-

---

* And again on page 415, Vol. II, he observes—"I am persuaded that, if it were to be put to the vote among the people of Oudh, ninety-nine in a hundred would rather remain as they are without any feeling of security in life or property than have our system introduced in its present complicated state; but that ninety-nine in a hundred would rather have our Government than live as they do, if a more simple system, which they could understand, were promised at the same time. In 1801, when the Oudh territory was divided, and half taken by us, and half left to Oudh, the landed aristocracy of each were about equal. Now hardly a family of this class remains in our half, while in Oudh it remains unimpaired. Everybody in Oudh believes those families to have been systematically crushed."

two villages, had been led to conquest by their chief Kesari seventeen generations ago; the Chauhans of Magat and Kathwara, under two brothers, Acharaj and Bacharaj, had ousted the Kurmis from their twenty villages thirteen generations previously; the Paonwars who, nineteen generations ago, had routed the Kurmis of Raepur, were in possession of their victoriously won property; the Nikombs still retained their hereditary estate of twenty-four villages without a transfer; and many other examples could be adduced. On the opposite side of the Ganges it is reported that 65 per cent. of the land in Cawnpore has already passed away to strangers.*

It is scarcely now a question which admits of dispute that our system of revenue assessment and collection does in some strange manner succeed in ousting from their hereditary estates most of these small independent landowners in whose interests our settlements are supposed to be framed; on this point the testimony of all officers and of all published reports unhesitatingly agrees; it is also the unanimous opinion of English officials that this is a grave evil, and that every effort should be made to check the rapid decay of the old landowners of Upper India.

The fact of the almost universal indebtedness of the hereditary proprietors of land is so candidly admitted that no proof is necessary; it may be desirable, however, to adduce a few instances of this rapid impoverishment.

---

* The landowners in the Lucknow and Unao districts are now described as being deeply involved in debt and difficulties. The Deputy Commissioner of Unao reported in 1872 that "the mass of the people is deeply involved," and the circumstances of the Lucknow landholders are described by Colonel Reid, the Commissioner. (*Vide* page 26, note.)

The revenue assessment in Unao was a fair and equitable one, and although a revision had been considered advisable, it has not been found necessary to reduce the land-tax to any appreciable extent. In Lucknow the reductions will apparently not exceed Rs. 15,000.

As already stated, it appears that in Cawnpore,* out of 2,311 villages, 69 per cent. have been transferred, besides a large number of portions of villages; and it is noted that "in others the change is merely a question of time." Mr. Crosthwaite, in his able essay, adds, that "to show the speedy rate at which it is progressing, it may be mentioned that in one subdivision of Etawah a money-lender, who had only a small share of a village thirty years ago, is now master of forty entire villages, and has shares in as many more; and, to whatever part of the country we turn, much the same story meets us. From the Punjab, from Bombay, from Central India, everywhere the ancient owners of the soil are giving place to the trader and the usurer."†

Although Mr. Crosthwaite is in error in supposing that "the class of ex-proprietors is our own work, the offspring of our own laws," that is to say, that transfers were unknown in the days of native rule, it is plain that the ruin of the proprietors of landed estates proceeds at terrible speed, when once the English Government has taken a district or a province under its care.

It seems that when the Jhansi district was last assessed, the settlement officer found that 13 per cent. of the land in that district had changed hands, although, "owing partly to the exertions of the local officers, and partly to the ignorance of the people of the change in the law, sales in actual execution of debt had been hitherto avoided." When this was penned, however, auction-sales had commenced, and

* "A Land Policy for Northern India." Vol. 53, *Calcutta Review*, page 209, 1873.

† In April 1871, the Chief Commissioner of the Central Provinces addressed the Government of India on the subject of these transfers; since then he has submitted a further report on the subject, and he remarks that the evil is daily increasing. In his opinion the time has arrived for "early legislation, which must terminate for years all further discussion." He considers the circumstances of those provinces in regard to these transfers as exceptional.

it is to be feared, therefore, that transfers will now increase with still greater speed.*

In regard to the old districts of the N. W. Provinces Mr. Crosthwaite records that it is not necessary to give examples, for the facts are not denied, and, indeed, since the Government of India has deemed it advisable to sanction special provisions for the protection of the dispossessed landowners, further illustrations seem superfluous.

---

* Later accounts give a most pitiable description of the impoverishment of both the landowners and of the tenantry in the Jhansi district, and in other neighbouring districts of the Jhansi division their condition is reported by the Board of Revenue to be "alarming." The landowners are said to be, without exception, hopelessly involved in debt, the population is diminishing, land is falling out of cultivation, and cattle and farming stock are deteriorating. In order to collect the revenue demand of the Jhansi division in 1873-74, no less than 4,600 writs of demand were issued, 57 distraints and sales of moveable property were made, 21 estates were taken under direct management, 1 estate was transferred, and the settlement of 19 was annulled. In Banda 4,965 processes were issued, 220 arrests were made, and 193 distresses and sales of moveables were effected. Yet, as the *Pioneer* of the 24th August remarks, the Collector is said "to have tempered severe measures with discretion, and to have released landholders who could not pay, and whom it was useless to imprison." Much the same report comes from Hamirpur. In the Jhansi division the arrears of revenue amounted in 1873-74 to Rs. 1,24,300 ; in Banda the balance due was Rs. 29,000, and we read that since the mutiny the arrears of revenue in the Jhansi division amount nearly to ten lakhs.

Land, it is reported, has almost become unsaleable, and does not fetch two years' purchase ; no one will buy some villages on any terms.

Equally deplorable is the state of the tenantry, but it is not necessary to give further details. It seems uncertain how far this terrible state of things is due to bad seasons, to cattle disease, to farmers, or to over-assessment and to rigidity of collection.

It is noticeable that Mr. Mayne seemed to have prophetic vision of what was to come, when he recorded so far back as 1859 A.D. that "to raise the revenue (in Bundelcund) seems to have been the main object; and, let the means be what they might, so long as an increase of revenue was obtained, it was received as an indication of prosperity, and limitation to the power and possibility of paying appears never to have been contemplated."

It may be noted that in the Hardui district of the Oudh province, which has only been recently re-assessed to the land-tax, transfers of land have been proceeding at a most alarming rate ;* and in another district it is believed that within ten years of re-assessment no less than 30 per cent. of the land has passed away to strangers.†

A large number of the talukdari estates in Oudh have only been saved from utter ruin by the passing of a special Act, in accordance with which officers of the Oudh Commission have been placed in sole charge of these estates; the interest due on mortgages and loans has been compulsorily reduced to 12 per cent., and the owners have to content themselves with a moderate personal allowance, until the arrears of revenue and their personal debts are liquidated; and there is little doubt, that, but for the wise

---

* *Vide* the report of the Collector as given on page 40, Chap. III.

† The Commissioner of Lucknow also records in regard to the land-owners of a third (the Lucknow) district, that "very great difficulty has been experienced in collecting the revenue, and notwithstanding numerous alienations, temporary and permanent, by landholders to obtain the means of meeting these obligations, there is even now a considerable balance. Many zamindars, as noted by the settlement officer, are in straitened circumstances. But for this, no doubt, they might have pulled through a couple of bad years without borrowing, but the number of transfers certainly tends to indicate that the Government demand does not press too lightly." (Para. 15, Review of Settlement Report of Lucknow District.)

In Mr. Markham's Report on the Moral and Material Progress of India during 1872-73, which was presented to Parliament in June 1874, it is stated on page 139 that, during the year under review, the number of documents registered in the N. W. P. was 144,772, and 84,323 were registered in the Punjab; and the reviewer adds—that "in the North-West Provinces there was an enormous increase in the registration of deeds for the sale or mortgage of immoveable property, from 86,464 to 102,699. This is an alarming sign; but it is uncertain, whether the increase is in deeds executed, or in deeds brought for registration; and whether, if the former, the increase is due to the poverty and embarrassment of the landed classes, or to the rising price of land, tempting men to sell."

leniency of the Oudh Government in the last three years, many a small landowner would now be gnashing his teeth as a tenant-at-will with a shopkeeper or usurer gloating over his fall, and fattening on the profits of his ancestral acres.

It is not difficult to conceive the evil effects of this dispossession of the ancestral landowners from their hereditary estates; we derive an enormous revenue from the land; the solvency of the State depends on its prompt collection; the prosperity of our rule is bound up with the prosperity of agriculture, and of those who derive their subsistence from husbandry; if our system reduces the landed classes to beggary and discontent, reform is urgently required;* the spectacle of a desperate heart-broken expropríetor yearning to wreak his revenge on the upstart shopkeeper or avaricious money-lender who now holds the old lands, and who threatens to eject the broken-down bankrupt even out of the fields which he and his ancestors have tilled from father to son since they settled in the village generations ago, or to tear up by the roots, and sell at the nearest market, the old family mango trees, is one which may be witnessed in too many estates now, to allow a wise

* On this point Sir George Edmonstone wrote, that it is "certain that the old hereditary landholders do exercise an influence in their own villages and in their neighbourhood, such as the new men belonging to the mercantile classes can seldom acquire, and that they are consequently better able to support the Government in times of difficulty. In a political sense, therefore, it is for the interests of Government to protect the old hereditary proprietors in the possession of their ancestral estates, and to maintain in their integrity the coparcenary communities which are found more or less in all the districts of these provinces." And Sir W. Muir recorded that, "whether regarded by the natives to be right or wrong, the practical result of these sales has been equally disastrous. They contributed seriously to the embarrassment of Government, and to the confusion and disorder of the days of anarchy. They proved an eminent source of weakness. This is a fresh argument against the present system, superadded to the evils that were already felt to call for the adoption of all possible measures for checking the frequency of sales and permanent transfers."

ruler merely to sigh and wring his hands over the calamitous result of our benevolent intentions. It is impossible to count the number of villages to which Mr. Colvin's gloomy words might apply, when he writes that "there are villages within sixteen miles of the table at which I am writing where it is as much as the auction-purchaser's life is worth to show his face unattended by a rabble of cudgellers. He may sue his tenants (*i.e.*, the ex-proprietors) and obtain decrees for enhanced rents, but payment of these rents he will not get. A long series of struggles, commencing in our courts, marked in their progress certainly by affrays, and probably ending in murder, may possibly lead him at length to the position of an English proprietor. But in defence of their old rates, the Brahman, or Rajput, or Syad community, ignorant of political economy and mindful only of the traditions which record the origin and terms of their holding, will risk property and life itself."* This passage was quoted by Sir W. Muir in forwarding his draft revenue bill to the Legislative Council.

There is no wish to exaggerate the danger, for, discontented as they may be, the dispossessed landowners have never yet risen in united revolt against the British Government in times of peace; but let a day of general revolt again break in upon the calm course of our administration, and each ejected proprietor will at once, as he did in the mutiny, seize the occasion to regain by violence his old estate; on the day when danger assails our rule will come the opportunity for which he has long been panting, and he would be more than human if he failed to seize it; even now riots and affrays must frequently occur, when villages like those described by Mr. Colvin abound in every district.

If our system is in any way to blame for these evils, it must be reformed, and that speedily; it is not sufficient

* Cf. A. Colvin's Memorandum on Revision of N. W. P. Settlements, p. 114. Allahabad, 1872.

that we should rest content with the revenue policy of the Local Government of the North-West Provinces, calmly regard these transfers of land as unevitable, and deem that we satisfy the demands of justice by securing certain privileges in the shape of fixed favorable rents for the dispossessed landholder, whose loss of property, is admittedly attributable in a great measure to our unsuitable system of Government.* If it is true, as Mr. Bayley said in the Legislative Council, that "the sympathy which was shown to them (the ex-proprietors), not only during the mutiny, but at all times, by the general community, was in a great measure attributable to the feeling that they had been ruined, not by their own fault, but in a large degree by causes over which they had no control, and which was set down with some justice to the errors and failures of the British Government;" and if these errors and failures still continue to darken the success of our administration, then the rulers of this country should strain every nerve to wipe away this cause of reproach.

One word more. It must not be supposed that the new landowners are capitalists with the means, the knowledge, and the will to increase the productiveness of land, and to introduce improvement in agriculture; capitalists many of them indeed are, but that is all; their arrival does not mean the displacement of ruined and absentee Irish landlords by men of agricultural skill and enterprise; the

---

* Sir George Edmonstone recorded as follows on this point—"It cannot be denied that during the disturbance of 1857-58 the auction-purchasers of landed estates in these provinces were generally ejected from the possession of their acquired rights by the former proprietors, and from this the discontent and disloyalty of the latter may be inferentially ascribed to the direct and constant action of Government institutions in depriving them of their ancient possessions," though he considered that the possible exclusion of the interloping purchasers could not have been attributable to the operation of this cause only. (Quoted by Mr. Crosthwaite in his article above mentioned.)

new owner rarely, if ever, visits his estate; his life is that of the indolent city money-lender; he has no thought of his newly acquired lands, but how he may screw a larger rental out of the tillers of the soil. On this point there is no difference of opinion among those best qualified to judge. Mr. Crosthwaite remarks:—"I have seen a good many districts of the North-West Provinces, and it has been my fate to plod laboriously over hundreds of estates. I cannot call to mind a single instance in which one of these capitalist landlords did anything to improve his estate or better his tenantry. I think what has been my experience is the experience of the whole settlement staff."* He quotes also Mr. Justice Melvill's words that "the great object of the money-lender is to get the land into his own hands; and when he has succeeded, he is the worst possible landlord, spending nothing on the improvement of his estate, and rack-renting the unfortunate ryot, whose proprietary right has passed from him, but who is willing to slave for the usurer, rather than to abandon the field of his fathers. Any measure which tends to the general transfer of rights in land from the cultivating to the money-lending classes should, in my opinion, be viewed with the greatest jealousy."†

It will be well therefore now to examine in some detail the causes which are contributing to the ruin of the old landed proprietors; many of them may, no doubt, be considered as a "tale thrice told," but it will be advantageous to group them together before passing on to consider what remedies can be devised to check the spread of these evils.

---

* I only know one, an intelligent Lucknow lawyer, who has bought some fifteen villages, and is doing his best to improve them by the construction of wells, &c., while he treats his tenants with consideration.

† Page 209, Mr. Justice Melvill, High Court, Bombay. This was apparently part of a judgment delivered in the High Court.

CHAPTER II.

OUR MODE OF ASSESSMENT OF THE LAND REVENUE.

'A trembling contribution! why, we take
From every tree lop, bark, and part o' the timber;
And, though we leave it with a root, thus hack'd,
The crow will drink the sap."

MR. CROSTHWAITE, in his able and interesting essay,* entitled "A Land Policy for Northern India," remarks—that, "if the pressure of our revenue system drives the landowners into debt, it must be from one of two causes; either the assessment is immoderately high, or our system of collection must be bad. There is no third cause that can exist." And in regard to the assessment, he goes on to note that in his opinion it can hardly be maintained that the assessments have been high during the last twenty years in the North-Western Provinces.†

---

* *Calcutta Review*, number cxii.

† In the North-Western Provinces, Oudh, the Central Provinces, and the Punjab, the land-tax is fixed for thirty years only; while in Lower Bengal there is, as is well known, the permanent settlement of Lord Cornwallis; at the end of every thirty years the land-tax of the above-mentioned provinces is therefore revised and re-assessed.

At the time of settlement, the settlement officer, who is merely one of the covenanted civilians, military or uncovenanted officers belonging to the commission, has first to determine the Government revenue for the next thirty years; and, secondly, to prepare a complete record of all existing rights in the land.

In Oudh, as all titles in land were in a state of great chaos at annexation, the settlement officers and their assistants sat as civil courts of justice for the purpose of determining by formal suits the right of all claimants to every plot of land within the province.

In many cases, also, the Collector carried out this work in addition to his own current duties. Oudh officers have been and are still the hardest worked officials in all India.

On the other hand, there are many who think, in opposition to this view, that the severity of our assessments is one of the main causes of the embarrassments of the landowners of Northern India. There will be very little difficulty in showing that this view is to a great extent correct, and that a crushing land taxation in recent settlements has in many districts only too effectually lent its aid to the other causes which are now operating to complete the ruin of the hereditary land-proprietors.

The alleged severity of our assessment may either mean that the exaction of a payment of half the rental of an estate is in itself too heavy a demand, or that the Local Governments and their assessors fail to act up to the directions of superior authority, and either in ignorance, or from a deliberate choice, fix a demand, which is in fact considerably above half the actual rent-roll of the assessed property.

It has never yet been shown that a fair estimate of half assets is in itself too severe a demand. If we restricted our revenue demand to 50 per cent. of the actual rental, the tax would be fair enough; but we add to it the cesses and the cash wages of the village accountant and the village police; the 50 per cent. therefore represents only a part of the annual sum levied from the owners of land. Obviously, too much depends on the construction placed upon the word "assets" by the settlement officers and their superiors; if by "assets" it is signified that the assessment will be based on a fair computation of the annual sums which the landowners can, on the average, *collect*, there seems no reason to suppose that proprietors, whose estates are of the ordinary type, could not without much difficulty yearly pay in half their collections to the State.

In certain cases, where, for instance, the proprietary body has largely increased since last settlement, the payment of such a large proportion of the assets must press them with some severity: similarly, on estates where a great part of the land is held in sub-settlement by various classes of under-proprietors, who intercept a large share of the profits, both the landowner and his sub-holder, no doubt, find it difficult to exist on the small margin left for their respective support. Again, where it is found that, owing to the lightness of the expiring settlement, the enhancement will inevitably be very large, the new tax, even if a fair computation of half the rental, will seriously embarrass the tax-payer; but these special cases will be considered separately; at present an attempt will be made to show that in a great many districts the assessment has been fixed at a rate which is far above the actual half of the rent-roll.

It cannot now be denied that, owing to the financial crisis* of unhappy memory, to the outcries of a part of

* Mr. A. Colvin's memo., p. 129:—"Finally the financial panic occurred. Originating in the belief that money now abounded in these provinces, that the provinces particularly needed further expenditure for their own protection, and that the general wants of the State exceeded its income, these grew and rapidly strengthened a conviction that the present assessments of the North-Western Provinces were inadequate, and that the State was not receiving its proper share of the public revenue. The views of 1861 fell into discredit, and great pressure was put upon public officers to show cause why their calculations should not lead to the assumption of a larger rental."

In Oudh we read that "in Kheri much of the trouble is to be ascribed to the fact that here, as in parts of Gondah and Fyzabad, operations were pushed on with more haste than were perhaps advisable, in order to secure the Government an enhanced revenue as soon as possible." (P. 26, Oudh Revenue Report, 1873.)

Again on page 18 it is noted in regard to Fyzabad, that "it was found that in 1860 a circular was issued directing that, if the revised jama was declared on or after the 15th January in any given year, it was not to be demanded till the kharif of the following year; that is to say, a jama declared on the 15th January 1869 was not to be enforced until November 1870. It was also found that, on the occurrence of the financial panic in 1869, the Chief Commissioner, loyally doing his utmost to assist the Government of India, directed this rule to be disregarded in the parganas which were assessed at that time, and that its principle had generally not been followed throughout the district; and the revised jama was collected from the kharif immediately following the date of its declaration, so that the year of grace prescribed by the circular above referred to, and the policy of which will not perhaps be questioned, was denied to the agriculturists." (*Ibid*, page 19.)

the Indian Press,* and to the scarcely concealed qualification with which the rulers of provinces received the tidings of a largely increased revenue, settlement officers have been led to greatly exceed the 50 per cent. limit; and that they have, by assuming far too high average rent-rates, by setting up excessively high standards of the value and fertility of the different classes of soil, by speculating wildly on a prospective increase of the rentals, fixed the land-tax of many districts at figures which are considerably in excess of the half of the actual rent-roll.

No better proof of these severe assessments can be adduced than that afforded by Sir W. Muir himself in a memorandum penned by him in March 1874, which was published in the *Indian Economist* of the 30th June. Sir W. Muir, after commenting on the loud complaints, *ubique luctus ubique pavor,* which greeted him during his last cold-weather tour in those districts, in which revised assessments had been recently introduced,† proceeds to note that

* In regard to the views enunciated by the *Indian Economist*, a short and summary account will be found on page 73 of Mr. Colvin's memo.

† Sir W. Muir is noticing that one of the benefits which he had previously held in a recorded minute of 1861 to be likely to result from a permanent settlement was "content and satisfaction among the people;" and he proceeds to add, that he has seen cause of late to attach a higher importance even than he did before to the reason in favor of such a settlement, for "whenever his camp passed through districts in which the land-tax had lately been materially increased, the Lieutenant-Governor was assailed by bitter complaints of loss and hardship among the people: and it cannot be otherwise. The land-owners had during a whole generation enjoyed a certain income, and the expense of their families and retainers had long become adjusted thereto. Now, when it was suddenly cut down, the outgoings could not be readily adjusted to the new income, and want and hardship must press somewhere. The discontent was not decreased by seeing some of their neighbours, who seemed to get along very comfortably under the old settlement, receive an unexpected increase to their incomes by the diminution of their payments to Government. The increase of the land revenue was followed generally by a corresponding increase of

the pressure of the tax is undoubtedly heavier in some districts than in others, and in some parts even of the same district than in other subdivisions, and that in some districts the settlement officers have admittedly fixed the land revenue at a rate which is considerably above the actual half assets.

He writes:—"There is also another cause of variation in the pressure of the Government demand, and that is the varying standards which settlement officers have set before them in assessing the land revenue. But even with this check (a preliminary report), the assessment is so much dependent on the idiosyncrasy of the settlement officers, that one will be found assessing at a severer standard than another, and even the same officer himself on somewhat different standards at different times. There can, for example, be little doubt that the strong declamations of a part of the public press against the supposed tendency to under-assess had the effect at one period of inclining the balance and of leading some officers to press their assessments to a higher point than they would ortherwise have done. Again, some officers have, as they say, 'discounted the coming rise of rent,' that is, have pitched their standard rates at a level somewhat above the actual rental of the district, in the expectation that it would rise to the level assumed by them. This has been rightly discouraged by the Board of Revenue. To some extent, indeed, the principle has been admitted,—that is to say, settlement officers have been allowed to assume, when in any tract they find a prevailing rate, that exceptional cases of a lower rating will rise to such prevailing standard. But the Lieutenant-Governor fears that, in some cases, the action of the settlement officer has gone beyond this principle. For

---

rent, and the discontented cultivators added their cries to those of the landlords. The intensity of dissatisfaction and complaint, and the urgency of great bodies of petitioners pressing round the Lieutenant-Governor on these occasions, have been quite exceptional, only equalled indeed or surpassed by the declamation against the income-tax."

example, in the reports submitted, Mr. C. H. Crosthwaite states 'that he feels sure his assessments are nearer two-thirds than half the existing assets,'—*i.e.*, of the rental as they now stand. The same is said by Mr. Buck (though perhaps on insufficient grounds) of the assessments of Furruckabad; so also Mr. Ridsdale admits that his 'new assumed rental is at present in excess of the actual by 18 per cent.' On the other hand, the standard of assessment is in some districts admittedly low."

The late Lieutenant-Governor proceeds then to say, that it might be enquired why a revision of these assessments was not ordered, and his reasons for not rectifying the mistakes made in these assessment operations are thus given:—"The revision of a settlement deliberately made and provisionally engaged for by the people involves serious consideration; where the rates of rent have risen since settlement (as in Boolundshuhur) revision would hardly be fair, as the rise was enforced by the landlord in the expectation that the Government assessment would stand. In other cases, lapse of time and the inexpediency of unsettling agricultural interests have dictated the propriety of confirming settlements which might possibly have been rated at a higher demand. In a few cases, as in the eastern half of Moozuffernuggur and part of Jaloun, an entire revision has been enforced by Government; but, as a rule, it has been held inexpedient to disturb the settlement concluded and engaged for, except on the strongest grounds. But the resettlement of three and a half millions sterling of land revenue, spread as it has been over twelve or fifteen years, is a gigantic undertaking, and from the nature of the work, as above explained, it is certain that there have been great variations in different districts, and even in different parts of the same district, as to the pressure of the reveuue."

Here, then, a statesman, who has been—and, doubtless, deservedly—called one of the greatest revenue authorities in India, frankly admits the grave imperfections—nay, it may almost be said, the complete collapse—of the existing system of assessment. Although the ablest and most diligent of the N. W. P. civilians have been toiling for years to effect a proper revision of the land-tax, their laborious efforts have borne this disastrous fruit; in some districts the land-tax is described as immoderately low, and in other localities it is unreasonably high; and Sir William Muir was, it appears, only led to reject the idea of another complete revision, because he shrunk back appalled from the magnitude of the task.

Yet it seems greatly to be regretted that the late Lieutenant-Governor did not consider it possible at least to refuse his sanction to the assessment proposed for Etawah and Furruckabad. It is not easy to see how the reduction of the land-tax proposed for these two districts by 25 per cent., either permanently, or for a fixed term of years, could unsettle any one, and it would be an act of simple justice to refuse to permit over-taxation, even if that refusal entailed some fresh enquiries and some additional expenditure; it is difficult to comprehend why the landowners in these two districts should be abandoned to a rack-revenue, and the tenants to a rack-rent, because the assessors have unwillingly over-estimated the rentals of the landowners. In these districts the proprietors have to pay annually to the State a sum which, including the wages of the village accountant, the village police, and the new and old cesses, must at present amount to between 70 and 75 per cent. of their gross rentals, while the remainder of the rents must be swallowed up in legal expenses and in the cost of management.* Doubtless it has been debated, whether a revision of the revenue-demand of these two districts was not required, and criticism on a policy of inaction may appear inappropriate,

* *Viz.*, land-tax 66 per cent., village accountant 6 per cent., according to the N. W. P. Revenue Act, watchman 6 per cent., the cesses, including the local rates, 10 per cent. (in Oudh they are 5 per cent.), 77 per cent. in direct payment to the State, while 5 per cent. at least would be required for unpaid rents and the cost of management; after realizing the full rents, the owner would have barely 23 per cent. for his pittance, and no margin is left for bad seasons.

when it is penned in ignorance of the reasons which may have induced the Government of the North-West Provinces to hesitate to propose some modification of those assessments; on the facts, however, as stated by Sir William Muir himself, a considerable reduction of the land-tax appears indispensable, if the landowners of these districts are to be preserved from impoverishment.

It can never be a matter of surprise if, at the expiry of this settlement, the new settlement officers report that nearly all the land has passed away to strangers. Here, at any rate, is one plain cause for the embarrassments of the landed classes, yet the same Government which laboured so wisely to secure some privileges for the dispossessed landowner, has, in these instances, omitted to make an attempt to preserve to him his hereditary estate, although his ruin will undoubtedly be attributable to an excessive taxation. We should surely have expected a different policy from the speaker, who, in December 1873, declared in the Legislative Council (when considering the necessity of allowing ex-proprietors to retain rights in their seer) that "he could regard nothing as more unfortunate and disastrous than the course which from the beginning of our administration had been taken with the ex-proprietor; that the body to which we should have looked as the stay and backbone of our agricultural prosperity had been ground down to what he might call a depressed and emasculated tenantry—powerless for good, but strong for evil;" and that "it was felt incumbent to do all in our power to remedy this great evil."* Obviously, the first measure was to take care at once, as has been done by the Oudh Government, that no assessment was fixed at a sum which like this tax may entail the irretrievable ruin of the landed classes, and it might then reasonably be hoped that a great many proprietors would be preserved in the possession of their ancestral villages.

* The Bareilly assessment has been carefully revised, but the propriety of the land-tax of these two districts has not, so far as I know, been reconsidered.

Further proof need scarcely be given of the severity of the land-tax; if it need, Mr. C. Bayley's remarks are convincing. He gave it as his opinion in Council that "he believed he was within the mark when he said that, in the three quarters of a century during which our Government had held the N. W. P., there was scarcely a district in those provinces which had not suffered wholly or partially from over-assessment." In fact, as Mr. Mayne wrote of the Bundelcund settlement in 1859 A.D., "to raise the revenue seems to have been the main object, and let the means be what they might, so long as the increase of revenue was obtained, it was received as an indication of prosperity, and limitation to the power and possiblity of paying appears never to have been contemplated."

Just as in the N. W. Provinces Sir W. Muir found that he could not regard the assessments with any particular satisfaction, so in Oudh Sir George Couper has been obliged to reconsider the settlement of many of the twelve Oudh districts. There was, as it appears from the revenue reports of 1872 and 1873, reason to believe that in many of the districts the land-tax had been fixed at sums which exceeded more or less the fixed 50 per cent. limit, and the Chief Commissioner directed close inquiry into all suspected cases of over-assessment; he faced the certain risk of demoralizing the tax-payers, for it was clear, that, until the Government was satisfied that the demand was just and equitable, its officers could not, by employing extreme coercive processes, force the landowners to pay the full tax. Consequently extensive revisions in Hardui, Kheri, Faizabad, and Gonda were undertaken, and modifications of the assessments in Lucknow, Bara Banki, and Unao were sanctioned.*

* In regard to Kheri, the Oudh Revenue Report records that in a great many parganas, the rise of revenue proposed was enormous, and the landowners everywhere refused to sign the engagements to pay the revenue. It became therefore impossible to collect the revenue,

Having now generally shown that the proprietors of estates in both Oudh and the North-Western Provinces have been subjected to over-taxation in recent years, it will be advisable to present in some detail instances of the various modes in which settlement officers have persuaded themselves to fix these excessively high assessments.

The land-tax is, as a general rule, to be fixed on the basis of actually existing rents; obviously the State can only justly exact half of that sum, which does, or with ordinary care can be made to represent the rent-roll of the assessed estate; if the landowner wilfully allows his rental to fall below the standard of other properties of the same capabilities, he cannot expect the State to consent to forego its quota of the full realizable rent; except, however, in the case of an estate which fails to yield the average returns, owing to the undoubted negligence or the deliberate intention of the proprietor, the State cannot equitably take more

---

and the assessment in those parganas is being revised. The results here were therefore not ruinous to the landowners, as their stout resistance led to timely measures of relief; very different, it is to be feared, must be deemed the result of over-assessment in Hardui. From the Oudh Revenue Report of 1872, it seems that the Collector reported in that year that, "as regards the collection of land-revenue, we shall soon have a new set of landlords, who will probably be more punctual in their payments. From statements prepared by the tahsildar from the Registrar's books, I found that during the year mortgages were registered to the extent of Rs. 3,94,782-9-8, and sales of land to the extent of Rs.88,571-13-3. The total of both sales and mortgages amount to a third of the revenue of the district. It would be difficult to meet with a single village, excluding the larger talukas, in which the owners are free from debt, and the land free from encumbrance. I can affirm with confidence that the money, save a fraction or so, borrowed during the year, was taken to pay the revenue, and to no other purpose. The zamindars have been and are unable to meet the enhanced assessment."

In the next year, the Commissioner reported that in the subdivision of Kachandan, to which attention had been attracted on account of the high revenue rates prevailing, coupled with the extensive transfers of landed property, he thought that probably every village was over-assessed.

than the fair half of the average annual collections of the landowner.

It is manifest that if the assessing officer takes half of what he considers *ex cathedrâ* might under other circumstances be the full rack-rent of the village, instead of what is in fact without fault of the proprietor the existing rent-roll, he may double, or even treble, the allowed rental of the landowner with very little difficulty. Yet it is to be feared that settlement officers have too fondly relied on spic and span tables of average rent-rates, instead of basing their calculation mainly on the village rent-roll and on the special circumstances and condition of each estate.

For instance there are districts or subdivisions of districts where the high caste cultivators invariably pay at lower rates than those which can be exacted from men of inferior caste, such as Muraus, Lodhs, Ahirs, and Chamars; the Brahmans and Thakurs do not plough or till with their own hand, but keep ploughmen* and labourers to perform

* In the Gondah and Bharaich districts there is a form of voluntary predial slavery; the ploughmen of high caste tenants and the smaller landowners are low caste Hindus who have sold themselves to their master. In these districts local money-lenders and grain-dealers are scarce; hence, when a cultivator of the lower caste falls into debt, and has no grain-dealer to support his family with grain till the next harvest, he signs a bond to some Thakur or Brahman, whereby he contracts for a certain consideration, calculated usually on the amount of food to be supplied to the bankrupt's family, to serve the lender as his man until the debt is repaid; these deeds are regularly drawn up on stamped paper and are duly registered; the ploughman receives henceforth one-seventh of the crop for the support of himself and family. As long as he works for his master, he pays no interest for the debt.

These deeds are only recognized in our Courts as bond debts, but so old is the custom, and, to a certain extent, so beneficial to poorer cultivators of the lower castes in these backward districts is the certainty of a supply of food in the worst time, so useful too is the practice to the proud Rajput and Brahman, that it is not likely that this form of slavery will soon disappear. The ploughman yearly increases his debt; if he wants to marry his daughter, his master provides the necessary

all the toil of cultivation. Their wives, sisters, and daughters are debarred by their position from weeding and hoeing, watching and harvesting in the fields of their male relatives. It is clear therefore that they cannot afford to pay as high rents as those which can be exacted from men who dig and hoe without the aid of paid labour, and who are helped in that work by all the females of their households. Immemorial custom, the force of public opinion, and the absence of competition compel the landowner to allow his high caste cultivators to hold on favourable terms, and in many villages the best part of the cultivated area is tilled by these men; if no allowance is made by the settlement officer for the prevailing low rents, the assessment will manifestly press most heavily on the landowner; he will be forced to bear the loss himself, or he will have to strive his utmost to exact higher rents from the high caste cultivators; the village will be steeped in litigation, broils and riots will inevitably take place, and the struggle will end in the impoverishment and ruin of one, if not of both parties, in the decay of the village itself, and in the eventual loss of part of the Government revenue; the assessment must be based on the existing rents, in cases where the landowner is not himself to blame for the low level of the rates.

There is one parganah in which Brahmans and Thakurs compose 33 per cent. of the entire population, and till no less than 70 per cent. of the cultivated area; in another

---

food, sweetmeats, &c., for the marriage entertainment, and the cost of the supplies is entered in the accounts as a fresh loan; sometimes the master and man quarrel; the latter declares for instance that he was only given four rupees' worth of sweetmeats, or only supplied with food for five weeks, and not six weeks; if they do not come to terms, the master will often wake up next morning to find his ploughman gone; off goes the master in search of the fugitive; he usually finds him, and, aided by all the other high caste tenants of the village to which the ploughman has fled, and by remitting a small portion of the debt, or by promising a present of grain, he induces the serf to return to his slavery.

they count 31 per cent. of the population, and cultivate 70 per cent. of the land; and many other instances of a similar kind could be readily afforded. These men at least hold at 2 annas in the rupee less than the rates levied from tenants of lower castes, and in many villages they do not pay so much; they sublet a large portion of their holdings to Pasis and Ahirs, and pay but little to the land-owners; even where they consent to take leases at higher rates, they are incorrigible defaulters; it is of no avail to eject them, since, especially in the case of Brahmans, no other cultivators of low caste would consent to till the abandoned fields. It is a matter of universal experience in such sub-divisions that it is *impossible* for the landowner to collect from these high caste tenants more than the low rents at which they have invariably held their land. The non-recognition of this difficulty was the cause of over assessment in one district at least in Oudh.

In the same way the receipts of the landowners are much less in "batai" villages, where the rents are all paid in grain; here as a matter of fact the landowner scarcely ever secures his full share of the crops: much is pilfered surreptitiously by the cultivators before the harvest is quite ready for the sickle, and extra payments have to be made to the watchman and the weighman; in cases where the landowner is non-resident, of course his interests suffer still more severely. It may be supposed that all settlement officers bear in mind the obvious necessity of rating grain-rented lands at lower rates than those assumed for cash-paying fields. The quotations from Mr. R. Currie's report on the revision of the Bareilly assessment, which appeared in the *Pioneer* of 4th December 1874, show, however, that even experienced settlement officers forget to consider this point.*

---

* In the Terai tracts of the Bareilly district it appears that "the country is unhealthy and the population scanty; cultivation is careless, fields are badly ploughed, and the growing crop cannot be sufficiently guarded from the depredations of birds and animals; and often at

Allowance should be made for all causes which tend abnormally to lower the rents of particular villages; in a word the work of distributing the revised Government demand must be performed as laboriously and as carefully as the work of devising and calculating these, it is to be feared, often fatally deceptive "average rent-rates." Those assessors who reject the village rent-rolls as not affording any trustworthy data for their proposals are fond of deducing, as it is termed, average rates for the different kinds of soils. No one would deny there are certain advantages in this system, if it is only kept within moderate bounds; in most villages the cultivated area is divided into different classes, known by various names, as, for instance, the "goind" or fully manured land, the "matyar" or clay soil, the "bhur" or sandy ground, and tenants pay so much for each class;* a rent-roll therefore is readily tested when, after personal inquiry in the villages, the assessor learns what those prevailing rates are; sometimes of course the cultivators only pay at so much a bigha or acre on their total cultivation, and here the assessor would be unable to readily find out what rates any particular class of land fetched.

---

harvest time the tenants in these Bareilly lands are struck down by malignant fever, and are literally unable to secure in proper time or condition the harvest which has cost them so much to rear." The settlement officers had apparently applied the estimated outturns of lands more favorably situated in other subdivisions to these grain-rented tracts.

Mr. R. Currie, the revising officer, was of opinion that in fixing the land tax that "a maximum area of cultivation has been assumed as average and ordinary;" he proposed therefore that the average cultivated area be more moderately estimated.

* In other villages the rents are paid according to the situation of the field in regard to the village homestead; one rate is paid for goind, which is of course the land lying close round the village site, another for "manjhar," or land in the centre of the cultivated area, and a third for "palo," or outlying fields, which never receive any manure, and which lie too distant from the tenants' huts to receive careful tillage.

The tendency, however, of some officers is to reject rent-rolls altogether, and to compile most elaborate statements, showing a different rate for an infinite variety of soils, many of which according to village custom scarcely, if at all, differ from one another in their returns, or at any rate in their rents.

Mr. A. Colvin's memorandum shows one settlement officer dividing the soils into no less than thirteen different classes, *viz.*—

Gowhan 1st, gowhan 2nd, gowhan unirrigated, irrigated domati 1st, irrigated domati 2nd, irrigated bhur, terai 1st, terai 2nd, dry domati 1st, dry domati 2nd, dry bhur 1st, dry bhur 2nd, dry bhur 3rd.*

In this case it is surprising that the assessor thought it worth his while to introduce this elaborate system, since he records that by personal inquiry he satisfied himself as to the "tolerably accurate character of the village rent-roll." It is incredible that any assessor, whatever his talents or experience may have been, could have evolved correct average rent-rates for so many classes of soil, and of course by 'correct,' we mean that the rates assumed should in fact represent the actual paying value of each class of soil. Even if the settlement officer could do so, it appears absurd to suppose that the native surveyors can accurately apportion the lands of hundreds of villages between these different classes. The climax seems to be reached when it is described how, after already fixing the classes of "bhur" or sandy land, a third class was established for bhur, "into which all sloping land eroded by water is put." It is not surprising to learn that this is the Furruckabad settlement alluded to by Sir W. Muir as a severe assessment, and that the assessor of the Etawah district similarly divided his soils into twelve classes.† There is no desire

* Page 32.

† As an instance of an excessive taxation on the waste lands we refer the reader to the assessment of Faizabad in Oudh. The Chief

understood to discountenance the classification of land into certain conventional soils; attention is merely drawn to the danger of concocting such a multiplicity of subdivisions as twelve classes,* and of assuming different rent-rates for each class.

Settlement officers again, in the height of their zeal, peer with prophetic vision into the misty future, and they fix an assessment admittedly at the time above half assets on the assumption that, after a certain period, the rental of the village will from some defined cause increase to double the imposed land-tax. They speculate that jungle land will be brought under cultivation; that a canal will soon offer more abundant facilities for irrigation; that a railway or metalled road will give an easier and cheaper access to neighbouring markets; that prices will rise; that tenants will increase and multiply; that the rents are abnormally and absurdly low; that the land should pay much more; that rents could easily be enhanced, if the landowners would only properly exert themselves; and in this pleasant belief they at once raise the Government demand to a rate admittedly far above half of the existing rental, and this largely increased tax the landowners are at once politely admonished to pay.

Can there be a more suicidal or more grossly unjust system of taxation than this? The settlement officer calls on the landowner to pay up at once a half of that increase,

---

Commissioner, on page 6 of the Oudh Revenue Report for 1873-74, notes that, in the Commissioner's opinion, "the assessment put on waste was excessive," and there appears to be little doubt that this was one of the causes which rendered the breakdown of that assessment inevitable.

* These twelve soils were—

Gowhan 1st class (page 44, Mr. A. Colvin's memo.)	Good dry domati.
Gowhan 2nd class.	Bad do.
Do. 3rd ,,	Bhur ordinary.
Irrigated domati.	Do. bad in the ravines.
Inferior do.	Jhabar.
	Matyar.

which can only be obtained after the lapse of some years, and after the expenditure of much labour and of a considerable amount of capital. The cultivation of waste land is for instance a slow and costly process; the jungle growth has to be cut and carted away; tenants must be invited; the soil must be dug up by hand; outlying hamlets must be built; the families of the new-comers must be fed till the ripening of the harvest; and bullocks and seed must be provided; a season of heavy rainfall renders the mud huts uninhabitable, or a drought kills the crops; in a month or two the tenants have disappeared, the hamlets are deserted, and the land is again abandoned to grass and weeds. Two other manifest objections to such a system are, that it operates injuriously as a tax on improvements, and compels the landowners to plough up all their pasture ground. It seems to be forgotten that if the landowners are obliged in this way to cut every scrub of jungle, their cultivators and they themselves are left destitute of fuel; instead of using wood, they must now make all the manure into cow-cakes; they also obtain a scantier supply of fodder for their cattle, and the kine, deprived of their grazing land, grow thin, sicken and die. In a suburban district like Lucknow, the cattle are kept in the yard, and every scrap of manure is carefully stored away in stacks; in a jungle district like Gondah, they are tethered out in the fields, and their droppings enrich the soil; when the jungle is cut the area of cultivation is increased; but the area of well-manured land is diminished.

If the settlement officer calls on the landowner to pay up at once the full half of the prospective increase, it is obvious that the latter must be hard pressed even to find means wherewith to satisfy the exorbitant Government demand, much less will he be able to apply any capital towards the expected improvement of his estate; the assessor carries off all the available capital, and at the same time taxes the owner on the assumption that he will use it to improve his village.

To take an ordinary case. T. is a "bhyachara"* village held by a coparcenary body of Paonwars; the original land-tax was Rs. 372; the settlement officer, in obedience to the orders of that time, raised it to Rs. 700, assuming a rental of Rs. 1,300, and adding to this Rs. 100 for the culturable waste. The village lies in the centre of a large jungle swarming with deer, antelope, and other wild animals; the cultivated land consists of hard jungle-bound ground producing fair crops in years of abundant and seasonable rainfalls, but often in years of drought, or of scanty downpour, lying quite fallow: there are no wells, and cultivators are scarce, as the wild animals cause such ceaseless damage to the crops; the unfortunate landowners were called on to pay nearly double their existing land-tax, and Rs. 50 of this was obtained by supposing that they would soon bring under the plough the wretched culturable waste. Careful inquiry has since shewn that the actual rental had only amounted on the average to Rs. 1,100, and the heavy demand had quite crippled the owners; not an acre of waste had been ploughed up, and the original cultivated area had considerably decreased.

If any of the landowners of this country had taken a B.A. degree at the Calcutta University, they would assuredly apply Cassius' description of Cæsar to the settlement officer of their district:—

"Why, man, he doth bestride the narrow world
Like a Colossus, and we petty men
Walk under his huge legs, and creep about
To find ourselves dishonorable graves."

Again in villages where rents are perhaps low in comparison with those obtained from other lands of the same capabilities in neighbouring estates, the assessor without in any way aiding the landowner to enhance his rents,

---

* 'Bhyacharā' refers to that class of villages "in which the rights and interests of each co-sharer are determined not by his ancestral share, but by custom, or possession." See Messrs. Crosthwaite's N. W. Provinces Revenue Act, note to Section 44.

or giving him any time to raise them himself, at once adds 20, or 25, or 35 per cent. to the actual rental, and calls on the landowner immediately to pay up the full half without even a year's delay. This surely is a most reprehensible and most unjust practice: in no way is it intended to question the right of Government to share in every rupee of the rental, but it cannot be deemed just half of an income which has no existence save in the fancy of the assessor. Government fixes its demand for 30 years, and it is entitled to consider whether any great increase in the rental is likely to occur within that period; it is merely urged that to fix a demand of Rs. 75 in a village, where the rental only amounts to Rs. 100, in the belief that, at the end of a few years, the rent-roll can be raised or will have risen to Rs. 150, is not only in itself a grave injustice, but it is eminently calculated to prevent, or at least to seriously delay, the advent of that very increase on which the settlement officer reckons in fixing the revised demand. In many cases, before that period arrives, the wretched owner will have been inevitably ruined.

The N. W. P. Revenue Act authorizes the settlement officer to fix the rents of all privileged tenants at the time of the fixation of the revised tax, but he has no power to enhance the rents of tenants-at-will, who form the great bulk of the cultivators. In Oudh the assessor has no power whatever to interfere with rents, nor will the jurisdiction granted under the N. W. P. Revenue Act affect completed settlements.

It is difficult to understand how any Government could have allowed the assessors to raise the revenue, which admittedly is to be mainly based on actuals, to a figure which was at the time greatly in excess of the half-assets; the Collector had thus to grind the tax-payer for the payment of the half of a rental which he admittedly could not collect from his cultivators, until he had fought them one by one at great expense in the rent courts,—of a rental indeed, which, at the time of the first collection, had no foundation in fact. The position of the landowner and his tenants under this system has been well described by Mr. Inglis in his speech before the Legislative Council.

He said, that "the revised assessment on an estate was, however, not based on the actual rental then received from it by the landowner, which might be, and frequently was, below the fair value of the land; but on an estimate framed by the settlement officer of what the rental would be, were the rates of rent prevailing in the neighbourhood for similar land applied. Consequently it frequently happened that the revised jama* finally determined by the settlement officer was more than 50 per cent. of the actual rental then received by the landholder; but, as a settlement officer, he had no power, under the present law, to enforce the rates on which he had assessed at the time he declared his proposed assessment; the whole task and cost of bringing the rental up to that on which the revised assessment had been based was thrown upon the landholder. This took time, and frequently entailed a very considerable outlay upon him, as the demand might be contested through the District Civil Courts to the High Court. The landholder had thus to bear all the cost of instituting these suits, while, if, as generally happened, the ultimate decision was against the tenants, they were burdened, not only with the payment of the enhanced rent, but with all the expenses incurred in the Original and Appellate Courts. It seemed to him impossible to advocate the maintenance of this state of things; the mere statement of the results brought about by the present procedure seemed sufficient to condemn it."

It is astonishing, that a single settlement of the nature described should have been sanctioned, until at least sufficient time and assistance had been given to the proprietors

---

* Land tax.

to enable them to raise their rents to the rates fixed by the assessor. Thousands of landowners and cultivators must have been crippled in their resources, and involved in debt contracted at usurious interest, by these assessments. The State has here undertaken the part of a rack-renter, and in its greed for an early increase of revenue crushed both the owner of the land and the tiller of the soil.

Mr. Colvin describes the operations of the settlement officer in Pargana Baghput of the Meerut district. Here it appears that the rental had remained well nigh stationary during the last thirty years; "whether there were difficulties, which we know not of, in the way of enhancing rent, or whether the people were ignorant of the procedure, is doubtful, but the fact remains—*We do not find that rents have, as a rule, changed, and* " *all over the country, and especially this pargana, we find the low rents of olden days*" (the italics are Mr. Colvin's).

We are further told that the former rental had been Rs. 2,22,331; the settlement officer assumed a rental of Rs. 4,20,070, but he estimated the capabilities at about Rs. 5,10,000; if he had taken the latter estimate, "the increase on the assets of the old settlement would have been, not 88, but 129 per cent. But he could not say when that rental would be arrived at; and as he was dealing with men, and not with figures only, he did not dare to raise the demand at once to the sum so assumed." It is to be feared that a sudden rise of 88 per cent. will prove amply sufficient to cripple these proprietary communities and it is to be hoped, that the Collector has treated them with consideration.

Not only, must it be remembered, has the landowner had to sue in the courts to enhance the rents for his own profit but one-half of the decreed rent has, of course, gone to the State in the shape of revenue; yet he, and he alone, has been saddled with the costs of the litigation, though the State takes a full half of the enhancement. The assessor told him to raise his rental from Rs. 500 to Rs. 1,000, and without delay proceeded to fix the tax at Rs. 500. The landowner, after filing stamps and employing lawyers, after adjournments, delays, and appeals, obtains a decree raising the rental to the sum assumed by the settlement officer to represent the proper rental; he has probably had to borrow in the first instance at excessive interest, in order to pay the legal expenses; the decree transfers nominally the payment of all legal expenses,—but not the usurer's interest—to the tenantry; these crippled by this decree are either unable to pay the costs of the suit, or, if they do so, they are incapacitated from paying the enhanced rents; both they and their master have been involved in one common ruin; at least the State should have exempted from court-fees so much of the claim for the enhanced rent as represented the half due to the State in the shape of revenue. As to the heartburning and the bitter enmity created by these proceedings, no remarks are needed; the track of the settlement officer must leave not indeed burning villages, but scowling faces and griping poverty where before reigned peace, comfort, and contentment.*

---

* It is to be feared that many additions will have to be made to the number of those villages regarding some of which Mr. Colvin gives a dismal description (on page 114), when he records that "there are villages here within sixteen miles of the table at which I am writing, where it is as much as the auction-purchaser's life is worth to show his face unattended by a rabble of cudgellers."

It would appear also that in many cases, when the landowner sued in the courts to enhance the rents of his privileged tenants, the officers presiding took a different view of the capabilities of the soil, and in many cases refused to allow the required enhancement. The settlement officer had raised the land-tax, and had instructed the landowner to sue for higher rents; the unfortunate tax payer repairs to the Judge, and the Judge quietly tells him that the settlement officer was wrong, and that the rents cannot equitably be raised. Meanwhile the Collector sends a process server to arrest the bewildered landowner, because he has failed to pay the increased revenue demand. What must be the feelings of the tax payer?

It is to be hoped that, in the collection of the revenue, the landowners of districts or subdivisions in which the assessments has been thus conducted will receive some consideration and relief in years of agricultural distress, and that in future no proposals of this nature will receive the sanction of the controlling authority.

There are other noticeable causes which render even a revenue based on the half of the existing rental a very heavy demand. It frequently happens that no allowance is made for fallow lands, yet it is difficult to see how fields continually cropped can in this country only yield a continuance of good harvests; the assessor takes half of the full rental of each field, and it follows that the landowners cannot afford to allow any ground to lie untilled. It is a universal, and no doubt a correct, complaint that the land does not yield the same luxuriant crops that were gathered in the days of native rule and in the early times of our administration.

Again, in very few settlements have due allowances been made for bad seasons: Indian harvests are peculiarly liable to great vicissitudes and uncertainties. The agriculturist can never feel quite sure of his crop until it is gathered and stored on the threshing floor. If the assessor does not allow a slight margin for bad seasons (say 5 or 10 per cent.), a flood or a blight, a frost or a drought, will seriously, if not permanently, cripple the landowner. In certain villages lands are always liable to floods, as the fields lie along the banks of rivers, or align bogs and large tanks. On some estates there exist no means of artificial irrigation, and the spring crops depend entirely on the Christmas rain for their productiveness.

It will be replied that if Government makes no allowance for bad seasons, it does not increase the tax in years of great productiveness, and that in times of abundant harvest the landowner exclusively reaps the benefit of the larger crops. It is to be borne in mind, however, that, that if we fix the tax at the full half of the rental, even in good years the landowner only receives just that sum which he should on the assessor's assumptions collect every year; he cannot suddenly raise his rent in a year of fine harvests any more than the State can raise its revenue. If his full rental is Rs. 1,000 and the land-tax Rs. 500, then from the abundant harvests he only collects Rs. 1,000, and in a year of distress or partial failure of the crops he will collect much less. If his assessment had been fixed at Rs. 450 or 475, in proportion to the risk of failure in the village or estate, the tax would have left him some margin. This question, however, will be further discussed at a later stage. Suffice it to say, as an example, that the Commissioner of the Fyzabad division remarks that one of the causes for the breakdown of the Fyzabad assessment was that sufficient allowance had not been made for the precariousness of crops in consequence of the land being subject to floods.

It is further to be noted that in a great many villages there are outlying tracts of land, such as hard clay soil, land exposed to floods, &c., which are only tilled in years of exceptional agricultural prosperity; in other years the returns do not repay the trouble of tillage. If the assessor assumes for such ground the whole of the rent in grain or cash, which the landowner may obtain in an exceptionally prosperous season, as a basis for the future tax, he will fix a sum, which the proprietor never does on the average collect, but which indeed he only secures once or twice every ten years.* It is to be feared that the assessors have not been careful to compute accurately the annual value of this

* Under Akbar's system, as described by Elphinstone (page 542), the following classification was adopted:

1st.—Land which never required a fallow paid the full demand every harvest.

2nd.—Land which required fallows only paid when under cultivation.

3rd.—Land which had suffered from inundations, &c., or which had been three years out of cultivation, and required some expense to reclaim it, paid only two-fifths for the first year; but went on increasing till the fifth year, when it paid the full demand.

4th.—Land which had been more than five years out of cultivation enjoyed still more favorable terms for the first four years.

outlying ground, every acre of which is as a rule entered as 'cultivated' in the survey papers.*

There are, for instance, a number of villages which lie along the margin of a large jungle, sheltering armies of deer, pigs, and wild cattle, peafowls, jackals, hares, and monkeys. The land aligning this jungle was only tilled in scraps, and by fits and starts; all of it had at some time or another been ploughed up, and most of it had, when the crops were well defended from the raids of the wild animals, now and again yielded fair returns, but *all of it was never cultivated in any one year.* The assessment broke down, because the assessor did not make sufficient allowance for this feature. The landholders could not manage to pay a tax calculated as if all this land afforded them a yearly return. As they were taxed on this assumption, they could not afford to sufficiently protect the crops from depredations, or to give any aid to the tenants; and the tenants, compelled to pay up an increased rent, and obliged to watch night after night the crops growing on their outlying and defenceless holdings, deserted their homes and abandoned their fields altogether.

Reference has already been made to the various sub-holders, technically known as *pukhtadars*, *birtias*,

* In the Jhansi district no allowance appears to have been made by the settlement officer for the spread of what is known as *kans* grass. This seems to be the agricultural scourge of the part of the country. It seizes upon fallow lands, and it cannot be ploughed up thoroughly without intense application; it can be dug up, but the cost of this operation seems too great to allow of this mode of extirpation; and the Board of Revenue, North-Western Provinces, in their last report, add that "for the time being, the lands, which *kans* has occupied, are as much lost to zemindars as though they had been washed away by a river."—Page 15, Report for 1874.

It is not surprising, therefore, to read that Sir J. Strachey has suggested for the consideration of the Board "whether the experience of the last five years in Jhansi, and of many years in Bundelkhand, point to the expediency of adapting our system of settlement in the Bundelkhand districts more closely to the peculiar conditions of that part of the country."—Para. 8, Lieutenant-Governor's Review.

bisiwdars, &c., who abound in some estates. It is clear that if they are now compelled to pay a rent, calculated on the rack-rental of the land in their possession, they will be unable to meet their engagements. They were rarely under native rule mulcted by their rajahs in larger sums than those exacted from the independent landowners by the Government revenue collectors, or farmers. They had the same resources against over-taxation as their brethren the holders of revenue-engagements direct from the State.

If we assess the dependent birtia on a rack-rental, in other words, if we fix his demand at the whole assumed assets minus ten per cent. for his right *(hakk daswant)*, we fix a sum which he can, under no circumstances, yearly pay in to the proprietor. The costs of management, his share of the local cesses, and of the wages of the village accountant, and village police, and the arrears of rent due from the tenants-at-will, swallow up his 10 per cent. profit and leave him no margin whatever: he fails to pay the rent, and then the proprietor must borrow to liquidate the revenue demand.

As already noted on an earlier page, the estate of the Rajah of Bamnipair scarcely contains a single village which is not held by these birtias; and since annexation many of them have in their turn mortgaged various plots of land to other residents who pay no rent, but receive all the produce in lieu of interest. Again there is one estate of five villages, which is held by birtias, who are entitled to one-fourth of the gross rental, while below them is another set of birtias, who have been decreed the right to hold on payment of the estimated rental minu one-tenth. The landowner, therefore, cannot hope to collect any rent until the last set of birtias has paid the first body of sub-holders, and until the first brotherhood of these under-proprietors has paid him. All the birtias are in debt, and they raise money by mortgaging their fields to their tenants. Under our system not one of these sub-holders can be compelled to pay a penny until a decree has been given against him.

In Oudh there are also the sub-settlement villages; villages, that is, which were included in the sanads* granted to the talukdars, because they held them as part of their estates in 1856 A.D., but in which it was found that the original proprietors had, since the date of possession by the talukdars, held a sub-lease with some degree of continuousness in virtue of their former full proprietary title. Under the terms of the sanad such subordinate rights were to be protected, and all sub-proprietary communities, who could show that the circumstances of their holding under the talukdar fulfilled certain conditions laid down in a special Act† have received decrees for the possession of their ancestral villages on payment to the talukdars of the Government demand with the addition of 10, 15, or 25 per cent. of the gross rental.

If the statements made in these pages succeed in showing that the steady collection of 50 per cent. of the gross assets is in itself quite as severe a burden as landowners can bear, it is needless to observe that these sub-proprietors, who are of the same clans as the independent landowners, who have the same standard of comfort, the same habits, and the same characteristics, will with difficulty be able to exist on the scanty income allotted to them.

It is further to be noted that the talukdars have, by the laws in force in Oudh, no remedy against these sub-proprietors, save by a suit in court; that they have constantly to borrow large sums in order to clear off the Government balances on their estate before they can ever hope to get a decree against their obstinate or impoverished sub-holders,; that even possession of an unexecuted decree

* After the mutiny, Lord Canning first issued a proclamation, declaring that all rights in the land were confiscated to the State. He then gave a title-deed or letters patent under the seal of Government to the various large landowners, who were to be styled talukdars. These title-deeds gave the latter an indefeasible right of property in all villages, entered in the lists attached to the sanad.

† Act XXVI of 1866.

gives them small relief, since the Government is naturally reluctant to sanction the sale of these sub-tenures, which have been specially held up to public praise as instances of the rigid protection afforded to all subordinate rights at the talukdari settlement of the province.

Any attempts to collect the arrears by temporary attachment of the profits are a failure, for there are as a rule no profits to attach: the village expenses, the pay of the village accountant, and village watchman, and the cost of management swallow up all the surplus collections, if more money is accidentally received than will suffice to satisfy the current payments due to the talukdar.

It is also to be observed that these poverty-stricken sub-proprietors are now liable to pay every year a sum equivalent to the nominal demand of the talukdar under the native government: if they fail, the talukdar obtains a decree against them for the full amount, whereas before annexation they could fight the tax collector, abscond at will to the jungle or compromise the debt by a part payment. The talukdar could hold no immoveable weapon of woe over their heads in the shape of an unexecuted decree: all he could do was to hold the village direct, and try to realize the rents himself; but, as dispossessed sub-proprietors would probably murder his agents, and threaten to burn the houses of the tenantry if they paid to the latter, this system might and did frequently result in disastrous failure.

Our Government has rendered the sub-proprietor legally liable for an annual payment of the exorbitant sums only nominally due under the native government. The talukdar has to forestall his income in order to pay off the land-tax, while he has lost all the coercive powers which he held prior to annexation, for the prompt exaction of the sum due to him by the under-proprietors.

As a natural consequence the under-proprietor neglects to pay till he is sued, for he can only clear off the heavy land-tax with ever increasing difficulty. The talukdar must pay Government, and he has to plunge deeply into debt;

when he gains a decree, the under-proprietor, threatened with the auction-sale, similarly flies to the usurer for temporary relief, and so in a few years both proprietor and sub-proprietor are involved in hopeless debt.

It is to be regretted that Government should have practically created a new tenure by a virtual confiscation of a part of the powers and privileges of the superior owner. The spectacle of the constant transfer of the ancestral estates in the North-West Provinces might have shown as plainly, that, if our revenue system succeeded so successfully in reducing an independent landowner to beggary, it could not possibly succeed in maintaining such sub-proprietors in comfort. Had the Government allotted a certain portion of the village as seer either rent-free or at low rates to the sub-proprietors, according to the custom of the estate, and, as under native rule, allowed to the lord the option of granting a lease of the whole village, these under-proprietors would now be fairly prosperous, and certainly far more contented than they are; they would still be sub-proprietors, and though their estate would be more limited in area, it would be more remunerative in reality. Now they are burdened with the permanent possession of a village, on which the annual tax has to be steadily paid, even though it leaves to the sub-proprietors nothing except the continued liability to annually collect and pay up to the talukdar a sum amounting probably to the whole gross rental, except the difference between the favorable rate, and possible rack-rent of their own seer; their own small profits must be applied to the pay of the village servants and to the liquidation of the necessary village expenses.* Nor would the refusal have entailed any real hardship, or amounted in any respect to a confiscation of existing rights. Under the native government the large landowner had the same

* I accidentally came across a landowner, who had shown an unusual amount of prudence and sagacity. He was the solitary representative of the old Upadhya landowners, and he had to fight a wealthy opponent for the proprietary rights of the village. He found he was

power of holding his villages direct, in other words of temporarily cancelling the lease of his sub-holders, whenever they failed to pay their rents, and, at the close of each agricultural year, he had the option of renewing their lease, or of undertaking the direct management of the village. Their rights were restricted to their seer and nankar lands, and the possession of the village on a lease was not a right, but a matter of contract. If they refused to pay the demanded rent, their lord could hold it direct. We have passed an Act, under which all sub-holders who could prove that they had held the lease for a certain number of years within the twelve years preceding annexation, have obtained decrees for the exclusive and permanent possession of their villages, and their lord has no power to resume the lease, or to dispossess them of the management, as he had in the Nawabi.

In Oudh there has been other difficulties connected with the re-assessment to the land tax, and it is to be feared that large numbers of proprietors and sub-proprietors can trace their ruin to the action of the settlement department, as is well described by the present Chief Commissioner; —"In some districts, notably Fyzabad, Gonda, Kheri and parts of Sultanpur, at a time of supposed financial pressure, the revision of the assessment was hurried on, and a greatly enhanced demand was imposed before the settlement officer had had time to adjust the rights and liabilities of the various sharers and under-proprietors affected by the operation. It is not difficult to understand that a course,

---

being steadily ruined by legal expenses, that he had at the same time to pay Government the revised tax, and that his adversary was determined to get the village, even if he appealed to the Privy Council. The Brahman sold his rights to the lawyer, stipulating only that he should hold his old seer, which consisted of 37 acres of the best land, and his 10 acres of groves rent-free for ever: he paid all his debts; the lawyer won the village after an appeal to the Privy Council; but the Upadhya, with no rent or revenue to pay, is now known as the only "asuda," *i. e.*, well-to-do landowner in the neighbourhood.

such as this, necessarily entails great hardship on the persons directly responsible for the Government revenue and results in their frequent default. They cannot themselves meet the whole of the Government demand, and they are not in the position to recover from their co-sharers and subordinate-holders their fair quota of the increase."*

There is many a subsettled village, for instance, in which the co-sharers number over a hundred; the disastrous result therefore of forcing the headmen of the under-proprietary body to pay up a greatly enhanced tax, before it had been decided, what portion of that sum was due from each sharer, may easily be imagined. It must be recollected that at annexations all titles in land were in a state of extreme confusion, and that numbers of kinsmen who had for long been in service in the Oudh irregular force, or held posts in the retinue of the native officials and nobility, had, at annexation, returned to their homes and had claimed to be restored to their ancestral shares.† Similarly many others, who had absconded, or had been sold up in the later days of native rule, had returned in the mutiny and seized back their portions of the village lands. In most of these villages claims and counter-claims of all kinds, the hearing of which had been postponed till the commencement of the regular settlement, were therefore pending before the courts, and

* Page 13 of the Oudh Revenue Report, 1872-3. It must be recollected that in Oudh the settlement officers were simply crushed with work; not only had they to assess the land revenue, and to superintend the preparation of the record of rights in a newly annexed province, but their days were occupied with innumerable judicial cases, for they had to determine either as courts of first instance or of appeal the title to nearly all the landed property in their districts. In the early days of the settlement, the duties of the Settlement Officer and of the Deputy Commissioner (Magistrate and Collector) were sometimes, as already noted, combined in one office, yet the Oudh settlement is now nearly completed.

† Nor could their claim be denied, since when in service they had aided to defray the rent by continually remitting part of their salary to their managing kinsmen at home.

it was hopeless to expect any of these subholders to contribute much towards the land-tax, until their rights had been authoritatively determined. As, moreover, the sub-proprietary body was called upon to pay the enhanced demand, at the very time, when all their spare time and all their available capital were being devoted to litigation, it is not difficult to understand that "the action of the settlement department has, in many instances, pressed heavily on the people."

Lord Northbrook emphatically supported Sir George Couper's resolution to remedy these evils, and he authorized the Chief Commissioner to have no hesitation in reducing, either for a few years or for the term of the settlement, as circumstances might indicate, any assessment which was found in any way to press unduly on the agricultural population. It is to be feared, however, that much suffering, which cannot now be readily alleviated, has been caused by the policy of previous rulers, and that many have been irretrievably ruined by the injudicious haste with which settlement work in these districts was pressed to its supposed completion.

Under any circumstances the revision of an assessment entails great suffering upon the agricultural community. The income of every proprietor is suddenly reduced by 25, 50 or even 100 per cent., and before he has had time to recover from the blow—before he can put his house in order, reduce his expenditure, or raise his rents, the Collector ruthlessly summons him to pay in full the heavy revenue demand.

Surely those officers, who expect the proprietors of land in this country, whether members of an overgrown or even a small community, to be able at a short half year's notice to subsist on half their former income, are entirely devoid of imagination. They would probably urge that the landowners should have saved from their former extra profits, but where were they to place their savings? As a matter of fact most of them have merely multiplied up to the rate allowed by the extra receipts, and a heavy enhancement, suddenly exacted to the full measure, means a process of slow starvation. The question is a simple one. Is the State to sacrifice a portion of the possible increase for a short time, or is it deliberately to consign a proprietary body to ruin? There is no third alternative. There seems small mercy in following the example of the Meerut settlement, and in only at once raising the revenue 88 per cent. instead of 129 per cent., because we are dealing with men, and not with figures; a rise to the smaller amount means, as can scarcely be doubted, nothing but borrowing and mortgaging. Mr. Inglis seems fully aware of the necessity for mercy, since he records his opinion that one cause of the revenue arrears in Oudh is to be found in the fact, that such a large increase in the revenue demand, as was sanctioned in many of the Oudh districts, was at once collected before time had been given to the landholders to reduce their expenditure. This question will however be again discussed, when the proposals for remedial measures are described.

There is one other mode in which even a fair assessment presses with some severity upon a certain number of the sharers in a village; in a large number of what are called "imperfect pattidari" estates (*i.e.*, villages in which the cultivated area is for the most part divided between the sharers, but in which some of the fields and all the waste tanks, village site, and jungle are still held in common), it often happens that one co-sharer holds much of the best land; he may be a wealthy or a careful manager; he may have built on his share of the property new houses for new tenants, dug wells and invited the better classes of cultivators such as Muraus and Kurmis, to his fields. In other cases, although the co-owners are theoretically supposed to hold each a portion of the whole area corresponding to their nominal ancestral share (whether it be an anna or four annas, the village unit being one rupee), as a matter of fact the portions of land actually held by each sharer in no way correspond to the nominal shares. Various causes, broils, absence from home, or minority have contributed to this result. While one sharer, whose share is one-fourth, holds 100 acres, another, whose share amounts equally to one-fourth, has only in fact possession of 80 acres. The assessment of the village is made on the total cultivated area, and if the land tax is divided among the co-sharers in proportion to each one's recorded share, the holder of the 100 acres and the owner of the 80 acres have to pay equal sums, although one has in his possession 20 acres more than the other.

There remains for notice a particular instance, in which our system of assessment has pressed very hardly on a special class of the gentry of these annexed districts and provinces. Reference is made to the fixation of the revenue demand for the lands included in the old Mahomedan townlets, known as "Kasbas."

When the Mahomedan armies marched into Oudh at various dates, with the intention of conquering and permanently annexing the Rajput settlements, they invariably left a strong force at various points in the line of their march to protect their rear, and to keep open their communications with Delhi. These detached forces were encamped at various favorable localities, so as to command the surrounding country and the main roads. Both the officers and the men received grants of land round the small cantonment, and in the course of time houses were built and a townlet rose on the site of the old camp. The settlers married, cultivated the neighbouring fields, planted groves, marked out their family burial places, and constructed places of worship.

These small head-quarter townships are well described as a "Musalman settlement in a defensible military position, generally on the site of an ancient Hindu head-quarters, fort, or town, where, for mutual protection, the Musalmans, who had overrun and seized the proprietary of the surrounding villages, resided. Where the faujdars (commandant) and his troops, the parganah kanungo, and chaudhari, the mufti, kazi, and other high dignitaries lived, and, as must be the case, where the wealth and power of the Moslem sect was collected in one spot, a large settlement of Sayyid's mosques, dargahs, &c., sprang up. As a rule there was little land attached, and that was chiefly planted with fruit groves and held free of rent, whilst each man really had a free hold of the yard of his house, and the land occupied by his servants and followers."*

These orchards, small garden plots and cultivated scraps of land have been, since annexation, assessed to the revenue demand; their owners have lost now all the means of employment and opportunities of service which were open to them under native rule, and they have to eke out a miserable subsistence from the scanty profits of their minute holdings. Even had their land been left unassessed in consideration of their reduced circumstances, they would be hard pressed to find clothes and food. As it is, it is pitiable to stroll through one of these townlets and to witness

* Cf. Mr. Capper's judgment in the claim to the proprietary right of Kasba Amethi, Parganah Mohanlalganj, quoted in the Lucknow Settlement Report, page 35.

In the Lucknow district, there are several of these Kasbas, *viz.*, Amethi, Kakori, Bijnaur, Kasmandi. So also in the Unao district, the settlement officer records (p. 19) that there are several Kasbas "with a population varying from 5,000 to 7,500 inhabitants: with the exception of Bangarman, Morawan, and perhaps Poorwa, for in these alone is there anything like trade, these Kasbas are rapidly falling into decay; their prosperity was intimately connected with the native Government; their inhabitants for the most part made a comfortable livelihood, and the Government establishments brought traffic and wealth into them. Now these establishments have been removed, and the residents, having lost their service, and having for the most part no property to fall back upon, are sunk in the deepest poverty and wretchedness: with them it is truly the condition of the unjust steward over again. They cannot dig, and to beg they are ashamed. All changes of Government necessarily bring hardship on the discarded officials, but it is sad to see so much misery, and one cannot help feeling compassion for those who have suffered such reverses of fortune, though the fault rather of the system, under which they were born and bred, than their own."

the squalid poverty of these Mahomedan gentry. The whole town seems afflicted with a curse; the houses are crumbling to pieces; the decorated gateways stand open and defaced; the wood of the doors has been cut away for sale in the market; the poverty-stricken owners slink out of their houses in the dusk of evening to catch a breath of fresh air, for they are too proud to show their rags in the sunlight. The unfortunate residents of these small towns have therefore derived small benefit from the introduction of a civilized system of rule. Even in the worst days of previous anarchy, they retained their small holdings on a rent-free tenure; the English Government with its usual hard adherence to red-tape and regularity of procedure has saddled these native gentlemen with the burden of an oppressive taxation, and although they are now rendered more dependent than ever on their small estates by the very change of rule, they have been further reduced in their circumstances by this taxation to the land revenue.

It might have been expected that some special consideration would be shown towards this class of landed proprietors, but it does not appear that much mercy has been extended to them; they have been reduced to beggary and want.*

* In the Lucknow Settlement Report compiled by Mr. Butts, that officer refers to these townlets at length, and his remarks deserve quotation at length.

"Para. 85. But in certain cases the imposition of revenue has caused some hardships. I allude to the assessment of Kasbas, and the large villages that are connected with, and form part of the city of Lucknow. In all these, and especially round the city, which was the residence of the king and court, and the centre of a large Mahomedan population, numerous plots of land were granted for groves, or pleasure-houses, or gardens, and were always held rent-free.

"They were not generally important enough to require a *farmán*, not even when they were conferred, as endowments for a mosque, or temple, but, granted at the headquarters of parganahs, where the chakladar and his officials lived, it was sufficient that they were not assessed.

"So much land was taken out of the area for these groves and small plots "chaks" as they are called, that the rest of the land of the

Enough has now been said to make it clear that our system of assessment can scarcely be considered a success; indeed in many cases it has proved a disastrous failure.

A careful survey and an exact measurement of every cultivated plot and of all culturable waste followed by an elaborate calculation of average rent-rates for the various assumed classes of soil, and a conjectural estimate of the possible future assets of waste lands; one half of this estimated rental, educed or deduced from plausible, but frequently quite unreliable, calculations of produce, is fixed as the land-tax, and in but few instances is any allowance made for fallow lands, agricultural disasters, floods, droughts, or the poverty, and numbers of the proprietary community. Is it astonishing that our assessments prove a failure, or that in many districts they are steadily draining the life-blood of the agricultural population, both landowners and tenantry?

If our present mode of assessment had at least enabled the settlement officer to fix a really fair and moderate tax, strong objections could not perhaps reasonably be urged

---

village had to be distinguished as the *khalisa*, and in some of the city villages there is no *khalisa* left at all. These chaks have been bought and sold, and fetched large prices, as not belonging to the revenue-paying lands, though in the last days of the nawabi their sales formed an item of revenue, for one-fourth of the price realized was payable into the royal treasuries.

"But the survey and demarcation made no distinction. The village boundary was not yet forgotten, and the village was marked down on the map. The land was equally *cultivated* to the Amin (surveyor) whether it grew flowers, and oranges, or corn, and sugarcane. All however was thrown together, and the whole village assessed as a single tenure, and it has remained subsequently to allot the share of the revenue that should be borne by each *chak*. But this assessment has not been borne without much hardship. The land belonged chiefly to Musalmans, whose occupation and resources disappeared with the removal of the Court, and who could ill-afford to have their remaining resources tapped. But very many (in Lucknow) by personal inspection, and by placing them in the still unreached limits of 10 per cent. for groves, I have managed to set free, and for others I have secured a reduction of jama. I think it would have been as well of all these villages and kasba towns had been specially treated."

against the exceeding tediousness of the operations of the settlement staff; when however the results have been so far from satisfactory, a cogent additional argument for reform is derived from the consideration that in many instances more than a decade has passed since the commencement of the revision, and that the work of reassessment is not yet complete.

On this point conclusive evidence is afforded by Mr. Colvin, and his remarks may appropriately conclude this discussion. "Settlement operations," he writes "have now in one district or another extended over nineteen years. Lullutpore and Jalone were the first districts that came under revision, the work commencing in 1803, and not being brought to a close till 1869. Jhansi was begun upon in 1854 and closed in 1857. In all these districts the work was stopped, and much of its results destroyed by the mutiny in 1857. Thus in Jhansi the settlement of two parganahs were reported and sanctioned before the mutinies—the settlement of a third being also completed and reported. But before the order of Government had been received, the disturbances of 1857 broke over the country and swept away reports, settlement officer, and for a time the Government itself; of those three reports there is not a line now forthcoming. Copies of a considerable number of the village papers were recovered; but of the labours of the three years no complete record can be looked for. So, again, in Saharanpore where the work commenced in 1854; and 1857 found the measurement of the district drawing to a close. The outbreak of the mutinies put a stop to all ordinary district work, and to settlement work with the rest. In December 1857, it was resolved that the assessment of the district torn to pieces by anarchy and riot should be suspended for a year, and it was not till the close of 1859 that the work was allowed to recommence. It was reported in 1864, and condemned immediately; and the revision which was directed did not come to a close till 1857. Mozuffernuggur was commenced on in 1860; reported in 1865; partially condemned in 1867, and still labours under settlement. Bolundshuhur also commenced in 1860; was reported in 1865; was again in 1867 visited by a settlement officer, in consequence of the decisions regarding permanent settlement, and has recently been confirmed: after narrowly escaping in 1869 the fate of Mozuffernuggur. In Goruckpore commenced upon in 1860, a variety of patch-work connected with portions of the district kept a settlement officer at work till last year; but in the remaining districts of the provinces the work has been uninterruptedly pursued. What may yet be in store for them I cannot say; but unless fresh revisions are sanctioned, we should see the assessment of all the districts now under settlement completed by 1876; and the last district, Banda, of which the settlement falls in in 1874, disposed of in 1879. Twenty-six years will thus have elapsed from the date on which the two first of the districts now comprised in the North-West were placed in the hands of a settlement officer: others were begun twelve years ago, and are not yet sanctioned; one of these is not even yet completed. These facts are significant to those who know what the settlement of a district means; the value of property deprecated until the exact amount of the new assessment is declared; credit affected; heart-burning and irritation between landlord and tenant; suspicion of the intentions of the Government; a host of official underlings scattered broadcast over the vexed villages. I can conceive nothing more beneficial than a prompt assessment of the public demand with a speedy adjustment of rents and of proprietary rights. But nothing can equal the injury inflicted by a slow, uncertain settlement, dragging its length along, obstructed by conflicting orders, harassed by successive administrations, and finally threatened annihilation at the moment, when it seemed to have nearly finished its course. Little wonder that we hear of the land needing rest."*

* P. 94-95. Memo. on Revision of Settlements, N. W. P., 1872.

CHAPTER III.

OUR SYSTEM OF COLLECTION OF THE LAND-TAX, AND THE DEFECTS IN OUR ADMINISTRATION.

Shylock—An oath, an oath I have an oath in heaven;
Shall I lay perjury upon my soul?
No, not for Venice. I stay here on my bond.

The preceding chapter was penned to show that it cannot justly be affirmed, that our revenue assessments have been as a rule light, or even that they have represented a moderate and equitable demand.

Not only is it incorrect to assert that the land-tax has been in all districts fairly assessed, but an attempt will now be made to show that our system of collection is also faulty, and unsuitable, and that many reforms must be carried into operation before it can be regarded as embodying an unassailable method of administration.

Starting with a tax, which is in many cases considerably in excess of the 50 per cent. lands, and which in some districts constitutes unmistakeably a rack-revenue, there is too much reason to fear that our system is harsh, rigid and grinding to a degree, that we fix a certain sum as the proper amount of the tax, and that we collect it, turning neither to the right nor to the left with a steady, persistent, merciless strictness, worthy only of a Shylock, and not of a civilized Government.*

---

* In the N. W. P. Board of Revenue Report for 1873-74, for instance, it is recorded that "there is no doubt that Fatehpur is very heavily and very unequally assessed." The Collector reports that "it has proved necessary to use every coercive measure short of compulsory alienations of land to collect the revenue. In many cases, where considerable balances remained unpaid, the villages have been and still attached in order to prevent further misappropriation of assets and to protect the zemindars from their own reckless extravagance." But where are the assets they wasted if the assessment is so severe? The assessment referred to is apparently the one now expiring, and not the revised one.

It must be recollected that, even supposing the Government demand does not actually exceed half assets, we exact in the North-West Provinces 10 per cent.* (and in Oudh 5 per cent.) more as extra cesses,† we enforce cash payments up to 6 per cent. on the land-tax for the wages, both of the village watchmen and of the village accountant, so that the proportion payable to the State may practically amount to between 57 and 61 per cent. of the gross assets. It is further to be borne in mind that the landholders paid the great bulk of the income-tax, and that they were assessed not on their net income but on the Government land-tax,

---

* As to the 10 per cent. cess, the Board of Revenue remark that the imposition of the 10 per cent. cess in Fatehpur "came upon the people at a time when they were looking for relief at revision of settlement." There is no wish to reopen the controversy, but there is no doubt that as boldly stated in an official despatch by the Oudh Government, that the imposition of this tax, carried out by Lord Mayo's Government at the time of the introduction of the decentralization scheme, was felt by the landed classes as a great breach of moral faith on the part of the Government.

It avails little to argue, as Sir John Strachey does, that this is not a payment exacted from zemindars as landowners, but an income-tax assessed on them as ordinary inhabitants. The landed classes did believe that when they signed the revenue engagement, they would not be liable to fresh taxation based on their land-tax for thirty years, and the India Office admits apparently that they had cause for their complaints, since in the annual Review presented to Parliament in 1872 (p. 12) special mention is made of those cases, *viz.*: "In Oudh also the local rate cess has caused much discontent, and its imposition is reported to have been looked upon as a breach of faith in the villages." This is however a secondary consideration; the matter of moment is that they cannot afford to pay. Besides, if it is levied from them as ordinary inhabitants, all other classes should be required to contribute their quota.

† In the North-West Provinces, the village accountant's salary is provided for by the 6 per cent. tax on the land revenue (cf. section 30 and notes, North-West Province Revenue Act, Messrs. Crosthwaites' edition,) *i,e.*, 3 per cent. on the annual value, which is calculated as double the revenue demand.

The editors remark that "this is no new tax," but the compulsory payment of such a percentage in hard cash is a very different thing to giving the village accountant certain variable and irregular allowances and privileges as under native rule.

as if the other half of the rental was all collected and went all into the pockets of the landowners as income; of course 5 per cent. of the rent may usually be struck off as "bad debts." A fixed steady drain to this amount probably proves a heavier burden than the varying exactions of the native Government. Under a native administration the landowners enjoyed other sources of income than those derived simply from rent; they collected transit dues from travellers and from the carriers of merchandise; the kalwar or spirit-vendor paid them fees, and so did the lunia or salt manufacturers; there also was less drain on the powers of the soil; there were fewer mouths to feed; and they had relations in the native army or in service of different kinds, who sent their contributions towards the liquidation of the land-tax.*

Our system is simply to collect the tax to the last penny through the agency of the Tahsildars; as the kists or instalments fall due, the latter officer scatters his notices to pay (dastaks) all over his subdivision; there are no jungles to fly to for refuge, and there are auction-sales which are upheld by the arm of a resistless Government; the Collector knows little and does less; the landowners feel that mercy is not to be expected; they pay what they can from the rents, and they mortgage or sell their property privately in order to liquidate any balances, for they fear that a smaller sum will be secured, if the sale is an auction one managed by dishonest Government subordinates.

There is in fact no real revenue administration; the Collector, especially in Oudh and the Punjab, is a tax-gatherer and nothing more; he is a compulsory jack-of-all-trades whose days are spent in inditing countless reports on all miscellaneous matter of great or small importance, upon which the local Government of the day sets, or is forced to set, great store; he has to draw up portentous memos on conservancy, municipalities, drains, and self-government all the morning; his afternoons are occupied with his appellate

* The Oudh Government has lately issued rules for the better regulation of dastak-issues.

work, and an odd half hour or so, as leisure permits, is with difficulty snatched for the real work of a Collector, namely, the disposal of the revenue reports; those papers, which have to do with the future prosperity or ruin of villages, must be perfunctorily rushed through, while a proposal for a new latrine has taken up hours of valuable time.

The English correspondence and the judicial work *must* be got through for obvious reasons, but few know or care about the internal state of a district so long as the revenue balance sheet is clear; the registers of transfers of landed property may be long enough to stretch from Lahore to Peshawar, but few pay any attention to a trifle of this kind;* the revenue has all been realized without much resort to coercive measures, for the mere threat of a Tahsildar suffices in most cases to drive the landowner to the money-lender, and the Local Government congratulates itself, that the largest revenue ever known has been realized in a year of great agricultural distress without any noticeable resort to the sterner coercive processes;† *animam picturâ pascit inani*, for those who go among the people, and who really make good use of their cold weather tour, know how grinding is the poverty of the landowners and how many have been forced to borrow at ruinous interest,

* Reference is made, of course, to the registers of deeds kept in the registration offices, and not to the dakhil kharij (mutation of names) effected by the Collector in his "malguzari" register. These mutations only take place in regard to sales or usufructuary mortgages of the property of those whose names are entered in the Collector's books as responsible for the revenue demand.

† As the Commissioner of Fyzabad writes—"I would carefully avoid any representation which can lead the Chief Commissioner to suppose that the bare fact of the realization of the Government revenue is any true indication of the condition of the administration of the division" (p. 12, Oudh Revenue Report, 1872). And again—"It is doubtless the duty of officers to see that the Government receives its dues. But where revenue-payers have to borrow money at 24 per cent., in order to meet the Government current demand, it is impossible to shut our eyes to the consequences. Ruin, utter and irretrievable, cannot be far off."

to mortgage and to sell, in order to meet the relentless Government demand. So the years roll on, and then perhaps when half the land in the district has changed hands, the Government wakes up, and the reason is asked in surprise; a culprit is sought, but who can possibly be charged with the crime, for the head of the district has been changed every year, and each officer has governed on the old principle of "after me the deluge."

There must be a more direct supervision maintained over the Tahsildars, and a more active interference in their system of collection. These officers are allowed to drivel on with their notices to pay, for each of which a fee of twelve annas is charged, till the rent has been spent, and then loans are necessarily required in order to pay off the arrears of revenue. Promptitude in enforcing payment is indispensable both in the interests of the State and of the landowner; any failure to pay should be at once reported to the Collector, and measures should be immediately taken for the realization of the arrears, or for their remission or temporary suspension.

It is considered that, as a general rule, a good season and a bad season should be held to counterbalance one another; the Government takes no more in a year of abundance than it does in an ordinary year, and therefore the landowners are expected to be able to pay up in full in years of bad harvest. Even supposing that this is quite fair as a general principle, in practice it is quite unsuited to the character of the people; they have yet to learn what is meant by prudence and economy; they have no place to keep any surplus receipts; they have rarely, as it is, much to spare, but what they have, is at once expended in a long deferred marriage, in payment of sums due to money-lenders, in buying new clothes, or a few trinkets for their families, with men of improvident habits it is absolutely necessary to take what we want from a man at the time when he has the money; it is hopeless to expect payment at a later period, unless we compel him to resort to the money-lender.*

Our system is founded upon a direct and distinct refusal to consider the habits and character of native landowners. We fix a demand for thirty years, holding, that what we collect in that period will, on the whole, taking good and

---

* From the Oudh Revenue Report for 1872, A.D., it appears that in the year under review only Rs. 34,242 were remitted out of a revenue demand of Rs. 1,41,36,015: of the sum thus remitted Rs. 18,313 were allowed in Sultanpur in consideration of the damage done by floods, and in Hardui the current revenue demand was reduced by Rs. 10,103 on account of losses caused by a hailstorm. In all the other ten districts, therefore, only Rs. 5,826 were remitted, and Sir George Couper justly remarked that "he was not satisfied that in the past year of widespread loss the disinclination of Collectors to propose remissions was not carried too far."

There seems little doubt that this opinion might have been more decided in its tone, when the description of the past years' harvests, as given in this report, is read.

"A fortnight before the commencement of the year, there was a fall of rain—perhaps unparalleled in the history of Oudh. It was nearly continuous over two-thirds of the province for three days and nights. The floods, which resulted, were reported by the railway officers to extend to an unbroken length of 120 miles along a line of railway which traverses the province. The crops on the inundated area were in places wholly destroyed, houses fell down sapped by the floods, stores of seed grain were entered by the water, cattle were swept away, and in some cases the people rescued with difficulty in boats. Driving winds accompanied the rain, and the clay huts of the poor were undermined even on the high grounds. The damage done in the Tahsil of Musafarkhana alone was reported to be as follows:—the kharif crops were entirely destroyed on 38,821 bighas; 8,302 houses were levelled; and 1,935 cattle and 81 human beings drowned. The floods were followed by fevers in the north and west by cholera, and cattle disease in the east and north."

"The ploughings for the rabi were late and scanty, but the saturated ground sent up a luxurious crop, and there was every prospect of a bumper harvest. In December and January, however, there were recurring falls of unseasonable rain, accompanied by fog and frost. Peas in the eastern districts rotted on the ground; the mustard and linseed crops all over the province so wholly failed, that ghee became cheaper

bad years together, about represent half of the total receipts: our system fails, because it will not consider, that it is far easier for a native landowner to pay double in a year of double receipts, and half the required sum in the following year of agricultural distress, than for him to pay the same sum in each of the two years.

It has however never been denied that unexpected calamities entitled the landowners to relief; drought, floods, hailstorms, cattle disease, may, in a few months, reduce a village to ruin; the necessity for relief is undoubted, and it may not be denied if the calamity is reported and appreciated; but in many cases the circumstances of the village are not known to the Collector; the Tahsildar regards himself merely as a tax-gatherer, whose efficiency in the eyes of his superiors depends entirely on the state

---

than oil. Wheat and barley were attacked by blight or ran to straw. Sugarcane and gram however were at least an average crop, and redeemed the harvest from being an absolute failure. It was so far fortunate for agriculturists that prices ruled high, and such crops as they reaped sold well; but the disasters of the kharif and rabi succeeded in different harvests in the preceding year, and a distress prevailed, which in some parts approached destitution, and occasioned the keenest anxiety for the future."

This tells its own tale, and it is not surprising to learn that there was a balance of land revenue amounting to Rs. 5,86,349 due at the end of the year; still many must have sold and mortgaged their properties to pay up even so much of the demand as was realized by the Collectors.

It cannot be deemed however in any way the fault of those officers that so little final relief was immediately proposed; changed again and again from one district to another, with a small and overworked staff of subordinates constantly shifted like themselves, they would be more than mortal, if they could have found time to enquire into every case of arrears, and to propose a suitable remedy; it was as much as they could do to suspend part of the demand in the more pressing cases until they should have had leisure to make some enquiry.

In Oudh the districts are very large, and the population is exceedingly dense, averaging 465 per square mile; while in the Punjab the average is only 172, and in the North-West Provinces, 378.

of his balance sheet; he does not take the initiative, and no measures of relief are allowed; in a few cases some relief may be proposed, but the proceedings are dilatory, and it arrives too late to save the landowners from resort to money-lenders, while resort to the money-lenders at the usual usurious interest is simply inevitable ruin.*

Many instances could be given by every officer in which, owing to the absence of any local knowledge or to an absolute want of leisure on the part of the Collector, harshness was involuntarily exercised towards revenue defaulters.

The writer recollects that a Tahsildar once sent up a general report in explanation of the revenue arrears in his sub-district, and although the great majority of the defaulting landowners had been ruined, or seriously crippled in their resources by the disastrous floods of 1871, which had simply converted many villages into swamps, this officer described them one and all as "nâdihand," that is, contumacious defaulters; in one or two instances he varied his phraseology by terming them "sharir," or law-defying

* The Tahsildar or sub-collector is the chief revenue authority for the Tahsil or primary subdivision of a district; a Tahsil is again divided into parganas.

The Tahsildar is in Oudh, Punjab, and Central Provinces a very overworked officer; not only has he to realize the land-tax, but he is also the chief assistant to the Collector in all the miscellaneous business, described in a subsequent note; and in addition he is overburdened with judicial work in minor civil, rent, and criminal cases; while this officer has in many cases small leisure to make himself acquainted with the condition of villages in his charge, he has lost the assistance of the subordinate who should be his right-hand man, namely, the pargana kanungo; under our system this officer has become a mere office drudge at the Tahsil.

As Sir George Couper remarks—"It is to be feared that that intimate knowledge of the circumstances of the various proprietors and village communities within his Tahsil, which the Directions assume, that a Tahsildar possesses, can rarely be acquired by an Oudh Tahsildar, who has much judicial work to perform in addition to his onerous executive functions." Page 30, Revenue Report, 1873.

scoundrels, because they had refused to allow his underling to seize and carry off the wretched crops of the seer fields, from the produce of which these poverty-stricken families eked out a bare and miserable subsistence.

In many instances the necessity for relief has been admitted, and generosity has been shewn in the remission of all arrears of revenue, but still ruin is not delayed, or even temporarily averted, simply because the relief was not given with sufficient promptness, not in fact till it was practically useless, as the landowners had fallen too deeply into debt to extricate themselves from the gripe of the money-lender.

It is to be feared, that the ruin of many proprietary communities, for whom a tardy relief has been sanctioned, can be clearly attributed to our harsh and relentless method of collection, and to the defects of our administrative system, which overworks the Collector and the Tahsildar, and leaves them no leisure to acquaint themselves with the condition of the villages committed to their charge.

An example may be given from the Oudh Report of 1872; the Commissioner of Fyzabad tells the sad story of an estate named Seharia in Pargana Mahadewa of Gonda; "Seharia is held by numerous proprietors, all more or less in debt and difficulties. Their lands suffered from floods, and the Government revenue had been greatly increased. The consequence was that after paying up one-third of the Government demand, and collecting what they could from the cultivators, they abandoned their villages, sending word to the Deputy Commissioner to do what he liked with their estate. The Deputy Commissioner promises a report of proposed arrangements for the future, so that it is not necessary to do more than record the fact."

As to the Jhansi landowners, the Board of Revenue record as follows in their report for 1873-74:—"It is manifestly impossible for the zemindar to meet a jama calculated on the rental assets of the year of settlement, where a very larger proportion of the land yielding those assets cannot now be brought under the plough without recourse to the village banker. The Jhansi zemindars have paid up year by year the Government demand with the aid of the money-lender (so the Board are assured by the local Officers). They are deep in the banker's books; any relief that is afforded in the form of reduction of jama will benefit the creditor, not the debtor;" and in regard to the causes of distress, it is noted that they are, "firstly, the mutiny; secondly, the great loss which the agricultural populations suffered in the famine of 1868-69, and from which they never recovered; thirdly, the inroad of kans grass; fourthly, the insufficient remissions and reliefs which have been granted, and the pressure which was put on the zemindar in the mutiny year."

The Commissioner of Allahabad writes in regard to Fatehpur—"The affairs of Fatehpur was laid before the Board of Revenue in my last year's report, and I have seen nothing during this year to alter the opinion I then expressed; there can be no doubt but that the pressure of the revenue is very heavy in many parts of this district, a succession of bad seasons and a heavy revenue are hard to struggle against. The imposition of a 10 per cent. cess of course fell heaviest on those villages which were least able to bear it. The consequence has been that many villages altogether broke down. Some of these have been relieved, but I doubt much if the relief has gone far enough; there are many more villages still on the verge of ruin, and these too should be relieved."

In regard to the Banda district, the report of the Commissioner was as follows—"The year under report was a bad year, the rain harvest was almost everywhere a failure; this harvest produces the greater portion of the food of the people. The revenue is always collected with difficulty, the people are poor and indolent, and inclined to contumacy; the revenue cannot, I fear, be expected to be collected without some severity. I am glad to see that Mr. Knox tempered severe measures with some discretion by releasing some wretched landlords who could not pay, and whom it was useless to imprison. I expect there will be several more applications for farm and transfer before another report has to be written."

The Collector of Hardui points out in his annual report for 1872 that the landowners of his district are all in debt, and that he can affirm with confidence, that "the money, save a fraction or so borrowed during the year was taken to pay the revenue, and for no other purpose. The zemindars have been and are unable to meet the enhanced assessment. There has been during the last three years a deficiency of assets. I have received information, that in three estates situated in different parts of the district a large part of the lands has been rendered unculturable by what I suppose to be sub-soil percolation."

Every Collector and Assistant Collector could give examples of ruin caused by the rigidity of our system of collection, but repetition is wearisome, and one would resemble the disputant *qui utitur in re non dubiâ testibus non necessariis*. Even when relief is afforded to the landowners in the shape of remissions of revenue, and although it is a condition that they shall extend similar mercy towards their tenants, the Government too often omits to watch whether the cultivators ever receive any consideration from their landlords.

Riding through a large village one day, the writer came upon a crowded assemblage of the cultivators, and on inquiry it appeared that they had, as it were, struck, or were organizing a general abandonment of their fields, because the landowners had exacted the full rents from them, although their own arrears of revenue, amounting to a very considerable sum, had been recently remitted in full. The landowners were of course called on to refund the exacted rent, but this could not be done without raising strong feelings of animosity between the tenants and the landord.*

The "joint responsibility principle" is another constant source of injustice and oppression.† Under the native governments the different members of the proprietary communities were bound together by the ties of mutual interest; if any one co-sharer fell into arrears from extravagance, or from incapacity, the other co-sharers turned him out; he gave up his share; or else he was forced to pay up the balance by a mortgage to one or other of the solvent co-sharers, and he went his way into the world in search of a new livelihood. Now-a-days the spendthrift

---

* It is most important to secure the remission of rents on the occasion of any remission of revenue. The North-West Provinces Revenue Act contains a special provision on this point, and if the village rent-rolls are only fairly accurate, the Collector can have no difficulty in protecting the cultivators; the rent-rolls would be inspected, and the remitted rents marked off. The Peshkar and Kanungo could then be sent to the village to inform the tenants, and the rent courts could be debarred from hearing any claims brought by the landowners in regard to these remitted rents.

Dr. Thornton notices, that "when remissions of land revenue were granted by Government on account of the famine of 1866 (in Orissa) on the express condition that the rents of the ryots should also be remitted, the zemindars, as a rule, did not give the benefit of either the remissions or the advances they received to the ryots, but continued to collect their rents."—P. 234, Indian Public Works.

† "Every mahal or estate is a local area held under a separate revenue engagement for the payment of the land revenue. All the land on such area is as it were hypothecated for the payment of the revenue, and the proprietors are made responsible for the said revenue each and all in their persons and properties."—Messrs. Crosthwaite's North-West Provinces Revenue Act, Note to Section 146. This section is thus worded:—"In the case of every mahal, the entire mahal and all the proprietors jointly and severally shall be responsible to Government for the revenue for the time being assessed on the mahal."

"The proprietors are jointly and severally responsible; so that the Collector may at his option proceed against any one of the co-sharers, and against all of them at once."—Cf. notes to this section.

co-sharer laughs at the headman, when the latter calls on him for his share of the Government revenue; violence is not tolerated under our rule, and nothing is left to the responsible head of the village, but recourse to the law court; he gets a decree without difficulty, but the realization is a very different matter; there are no moveables to attach, and applications for sale languish for months in the different offices, before they receive the required sanction of the highest judicial* authority. The Tahsildar has meanwhile called on the headman to pay off from his own income the sum due from the co-sharer, and this hitherto well-to-do and punctual revenue payer is also crippled.

It is so easy for the Tahsildars to enforce the full payment of the revenue by adhering steadily to the principle of joint responsibility. There is sure to be some well-to-do co-sharer in the village; he can be seized and carried off to the Tahsil, or his moveable property can be attached and sold. To avoid further annoyance and disgrace he will pay up the arrears, and the balance-sheet is cleared.

It is a great injustice to maintain the joint responsibility as a primary method of collecting revenue, when our whole system of administration and our whole body of jurisprudence necessarily tend to the recognition of the separate status of the *individual* as opposed to that of communities; we persist in holding all the co-sharers of an estate jointly liable, while our mode of rule inevitably has destroyed the pre-existing coercive processes by which the community could punish the delinquency of any one of its members.

* In Oudh and the Punjab no sales of ancestral property in land can take place without the previous sanction of the highest judicial authority. This is a most excellent provision, if only delays in the disposal of these references are strictly avoided.

So Sir H. Maine writes:—"If I had to state what for the moment is the greatest change which has come over the people of India, and the change which has added most seriously to the difficulty of governing them, I should say it was the growth on all sides of the sense of individual legal right."

In a vast number of the villages, the community itself no longer exists in its completeness, for some money-lender, pleader, or shopkeeper has secured one or more shares in mortgage or in purchase. It is in these days of agricultural distress also a favourite trick of the mortgagees to avoid applying for mutation of names in the malguzari register;* the wretched poverty-stricken mortgagors are left in nominal possession of their share; the irresponsible money-lender carries off all the rent, yet he cannot be touched by the Collector; in such cases the shares should clearly be transferred, or sold by public auction, yet it is much easier to call on some solvent sharer to pay up the arrears. It is quite proper to maintain the principle as a last resource, but it should never be put in force until all means have been tried in vain to realize the balance from that share from which it was originally due. There could not be a greater deterrent from habits of thrift, than to force those to pay who were not responsible for the default.†

Some writers ascribe the embarrassments of the land-owning classes solely to their alleged reckless extravagance,

---

* The malguzari register is the register which records the names of the proprietors of the estate, to whom the Collector is to look for the payment of the land-tax. According to the provision of the North-West Provinces Revenue Act lessees or mortgagees in possession do not seem to be responsible for the Government revenue unless settlement has been made with them.—Cf. Note to Section 148, Messrs. Crosthwaite's edition.

† As Mr. Bird strongly insisted in 1832, each pattidar should be made primary responsible for his share of the Government revenue.

and this is the most popular theory, because it completely exonerates Government from blame. No one will deny that in many cases the ruin of landed proprietors can be traced to simple extravagance, that is, the wilful expenditure of sums considerably in excess of their ordinary income; so far as it can be proved that this is the cause of any particular landowner's indigence, the latter's loss of his estates is rather a matter for congratulation than for commiseration; there is room for considerable doubt however whether there has not been great exaggeration, and whether persistent extravagance should not be considered rather a characteristic of the Oudh Talukdars and the larger Bengal zamindars than of the proprietary communities of small landowners.

Many of the large landed proprietors are recklessly profuse in their expenditure; no household accounts are kept; mobs of lazy and peculating retainers are fed and clothed simply to lounge about their master's court-yard; vast sums are spent on marriages and other festivals, on elephants and caparisons, on jewels, and on women, while the estate is handed over to the mismanagement of corrupt and tyrannical agents; the ruin of idle and sensual profligates is a blessing to the State, and any expression of sympa-

---

He advised that "the accounts to be kept in the Tahsildar's office should show the total jama of the rental, the amount demandable from each patti, and where all pay separately from each sharer of that patti, and the payments made should be credited to the party, on account of whom they were made. In sending up the statement of arrears, the Tahsildar should furnish a copy of this account, countersigned by the Kanungos, and also a copy of the Kanungo's counterpart account, in which the private transfers of the sharers among themselves, and the different arrangements are (or ought to be) recorded. The Collector then having before him a statement both of the person from whom the arrear is actually due and also the actual state of that person's share, can put in force such measures as may be expedient against the actual defaulter without injuring others."—Selections from Revenue Records, N.-W. P., A.D. 1823—33, pp. 443-4. Published at N.-W. P. Government Press, 1872.

thy for their fall should excite ridicule.* Until the Talukdars of Oudh comprehend that "it is no Basenesse for the greatest to descend and looke into their owne estate," it is impossible that the Government can ameliorate their condition.

It is by no means clear that as a body the smaller landowners, the Thakur, Brahman, and Syad clansmen can be so universally condemned as guilty of the want of thrift; doubtless there are many gross instances of extravagance. There lives a small Thakur landowner who allowed his mother to sumptuously entertain a band of 3,000 Brahmans and beggars, and who then at once applied for a reduction of his land-tax on the ground of heavy over-assessment. A Brahman summoned to a feast has a voracious appetite, and he has been known to consume Rs. 7 worth of ordinary food and ordinary sweetmeats in a single day,† and the landowner's expenses could not have been less than Rs. 1,000; yet the total rental of this village hardly amounted to that sum, and his own annual profits could not have exceeded Rs. 400.

The daily life and the household expenses of the small landowner, the owner of a portion of the village area, differ but little from those of his cultivator; he dresses in the same clothes; he eats the same food; he lives in the same

* An instance of personal extravagance is given by the Chief Commissioner in the Oudh Revenue Reports for 1872:—"The first village in which he encamped is owned by two brothers, who paid the chukladar of the King of Oudh Rs. 19,000 a year and who now pay the Oudh Government Rs. 11,000. Each has set up an elephant and rivalled the other in his style of living, and they are worse off now than they were in the nawabi."

† There is an old proverb quoted by Dr. Fallon in his Dictionary, "achhe bhae atae, prân gae nickal," and he notes that "this is applied jestingly to the Chohans of Mathura, who are credited with eating to excess. The charity of feeding the poor is outdone in the custom of inducing each man to eat till he bursts, by the offer of a money reward rising from four annas up to a goldmohur for every sweetmeat eaten on a full stomach."

kind of house; he keeps no horses; he gives no entertainments, and he seldom leaves his home. On certain occasions, as at the marriage of his daughter,*—he does, it is true, expend for him large sums of money, and this money is borrowed at ruinous interest; few as are these occasions therefore, they frequently cripple him for many years, if not for life. It is impossible to defend the landowners from charges of extravagance in these matters, but they are no worse than any other classes, than their own cultivators, or than the punkah-coolie whose annual income does not exceed Rs. 48, and who spends Rs. 50 or Rs. 100 on a single marriage entertainment. It must be recollected that these customs, in obedience to which they are compelled to plunge into debt, have descended to them from their ancestors, that custom is a relentless demon in a caste-ridden country like India, and that the natives, when they fail to resist the traditions of their clan, and the voice of *their* public opinion are more deserving of our commiseration than of our contempt. Those who hurl demonstrations of wrath upon the heads of the unfortunate natives of Hindustan, are those, who know little of the people, and who cannot understand the resistless force of old-fashioned usages; such critics have no imagination, and they will rarely be good rulers of an alien race.

We have sternly repressed female infanticide, and we have raised up nothing in its place; we have forgotten that this practice,† however reprehensible according to European

* The Oudh Rajpoots have to pay heavy fees to secure bridegrooms for their daughters, since the Rajpoots of other parts of India regard many of the Oudh Thakurs as illegitimate. Among some of the Oudh clans concubinage is very common, so an alliance with them by marriage is not considered very desirable in the absence of a large bribe.

† As the settlement officer of Unao writes:—"So long as the advent of a daughter certainly entails on the Rajpoot debt, and possibly ruin, as in an instance I could quote at this moment, so long as the public opinion of their fellows is rather for than against it, and their family priests tacitly consent to it, so long will the crime continue."—Unao Report, p. 27.

ideas of morality, derives its origin from the well-understood inability of the father to celebrate his family marriages with the necessary pomp; that it is a custom mainly prompted by deep motives of domestic economy, being in fact the deliberate sacrifice of one member of the family for the preservation of the remainder; that with the largely increasing population it is now found more difficult than ever to dispose of female relations in marriage; that the presence of unmarried daughters, nieces, and sisters is a perpetual mark of disgrace, and that illicit and incestuous attachments giving rise to grave evils are the natural result of enforced female celibacy.*

In other ways it is not easy to detect many signs of undue expenditure; Brahmans and mendicants may receive a grant of a few patches of land rent-free; a Gosain (professional beggar), begging at the landowner's door, may be well fed for a week and dismissed with the present of a pony for his future comfort in travelling; and hospitality is readily offered to strangers, but all these are rare occasions, and they do not act as a regular drain on a landowner's resources.

As distinguished from *extravagance* the landowners are also accused of *improvidence;* it is charged against them, that if they do not expend sums in excess of their incomes, they at least fail to save; that in years of abundant harvests they lavish their receipts; that they neglect to retrench

* There is a large clan of Gahirwars, who under the native administration were powerful and rich, for they scarcely paid to the Government more than one-fourth of their rent-collections; then came our system of assessment, and their land-tax was raised enormously; bad seasons followed; they fell into debt, and now it is said that there is scarcely a house in which will not be found unmarried daughters, sisters, and cousins; they intermarry with high castes, and the cost is very heavy; they cannot marry these female relations into lower castes, and they cannot marry them without the old show of pomp. Their cry is not that the land-tax is above half assets, but that they are being disgraced by the presence of these unmarried relations, and that the sudden rise on the land-tax and the bad harvests have completed their ruin.

their expenses in bad seasons, and that they have consequently no hoard at home wherewith to make head against a period of agricultural distress.

It should be remembered, in the first place, that, though they may more easily collect their rents in a good year, they receive no extra profits except for their seer from a harvest of special abundance; that in most years their ordinary receipts barely suffice for their ordinary household expenses; that any little surplus is quickly absorbed in helping to defray the cost of a too long deferred marriage, in purchasing a few new clothes, in replacing a dead or worn-out bullock, or in rebuilding the fallen walls of their house; it is impossible for them to retrench their expenses, when as a rule they live almost from hand to mouth.

It is true that the larger landowners might considerably curtail their expenditure, and that they usually neglect to do so; the natives of this country are not however the only people who ruin themselves by striving to keep up appearances; the phenomenon is not a rare one in an intelligent European country like England; it is also to be considered that it is far easier for an English squire to hide his rags and his shame, than it is for a native landowner; a ruined English squire or nobleman takes refuge abroad, and conceals his poverty from the world; the native landowner has to live in his indigence openly before the gaze of his county. There is no desire to justify his faults, but it is urged that all the special circumstances of his social life should be considered, and that in them some slight palliation may be found for his extravagant and improvident habits. That which is ordinarily termed wilful extravagance is in many cases merely the desperate attempt to keep up appearances on an income, which has been suddenly reduced perhaps to one-half its former amount by a heavy enhancement of the Government demand.

The difficulties of the smaller landowner are largely increased by the constantly swelling numbers of the coparcenary body; the causes of this constant increase under our rule need not be enlarged on as they are self-evident; the proprietary body has been swelled not only in the ordinary course by an increase of the population, but also by the return of those members, who had formerly subsisted in service with native armies, or at the petty courts of native princes; as these men now live regularly at home, their families necessarily increase with great rapidity.

The effect on the welfare of the proprietary body is disastrous; the new comers all demand back their ancestral share, and the area cultivated by the co-sharers is constantly increasing; most of the land thus held in the seer is rented at favorable rates; the assets of the area held by the ordinary cultivators on the other hand are seriously diminished; the village-headmen and the heads of the different shares find ever greater difficulty in providing for the due payment of the Government demand; the co-sharers cannot be readily induced to pay up their rents, and there are inevitable disputes in respect to the collections from the lands held in common (shamilat).

There is one village where the divided shares are said to exceed 100, and where nearly the whole village area is cultivated by the co-sharers, all men entitled to receive their portion of the profits; the head man of each patti (divided share) has to collect the rents from the different co-sharers, who of course are more refractory than mere tenants-at-will, and the lumbardars or headmen of the thok (or combined number of pattis) have to induce all the different head-pattidars to contribute their due quota to the Government revenue.*

* As to the number of co-sharers, the Unao settlement officer writes, that "the number of divided pattis in villages held in severalty are very great, the average number being 10 per village, and as the average number of sharers in each patti may be set down at 4, we have about 40 sharers per village; taking the average size of villages, this would give about 13 acres of malguzari land per sharer. The majority of these men have nothing to live upon but their little property; it is not

There is another village where the proprietary body has within eight years included 200 additional bighas of khalsa* land within the seer, and this new seer is all held by the co-sharers on favorable terms: the numbers of the proprietary community are ever multiplying, and, *pari passu* with this increase, increase the occasions for expenditure in marriages and other festivals.†

---

therefore to be wondered at their getting into debt, considering their previous habits and general dislike to work. The great majority keep ploughmen, and no man calling himself a zamindar would permit his family to work in his fields."—Unao Report, p. 67.

* Khalsa = the land tilled by the tenants, the full rental of which was theoretically due to the State, as opposed to the seer, or land tilled by the proprietors themselves.

† Sir William Sleeman records (Vol. I., p. 170) that "our army and other public establishments form a great safety-valve for Oudh, and save it from a vast deal of fighting for shares in land, and the disorders which always attend it. Younger brothers enlist in our regiments, or find employment in our civil establishment, and leave their wives and children under the protection of the elder brother who manages the family estate for the common good. They send the greater part of their pay to him for their subsistence, and feel assured that he will see that they are provided for, should they lose their lives in our service. From the single district of Byswara in Oudh 16,000 men were, it is said, found to be so serving in our army and other establishments, and from Banda which adjoins it on the east 15,000, on an enquiry ordered to be made by Ghazeeuddin Hyder some twenty-five years ago."

The Unao settlement officer notes that "the sharers in possession admitted many persons to a share, who would not otherwise have been able to obtain one; the only persons, against whom strenuous opposition was made, were those who had fled in times of difficulty, leaving the other customers to fight the matter out as best they could. I confess I fully sympathise with the objectors, and when I had to give a decree to such a one, I always felt that I was doing an injustice in taking away a share from him who had fought and struggled for it in times of difficulty and danger, without being able to award compensation."—Unao Report, p. 71.

It was not possible, however, to deny shares to those men, for "they were responsible for the share of the loss, after the manager had been sold up, but the manager took the profit in compensation for his risk. I am sure that every one of them would have been very much

Co-sharers, as is indeed but natural, now all aspire to an actual and active participation in the rendition of accounts and tenaciously watch over their own interests at the distribution of the profits; even those who under native rule bore the brunt of the struggle against the Government Collector, or the revenue farmer, who managed the common lands, paid up the heavy exactions, saved the village from compulsory sale or mortgage, took over the share of absconded pattidars, and paid up the balance due for those defaulters, now find themselves reduced to their original one-pie share, while all the other proprietors who fled from oppression, or who contented themselves with their seer, and left the management and the surplus profits to the one able man amongst them, now clamour and wrangle over every penny of the receipts.*

Simple bad management of their estate may often with reason be ascribed to some landowners, and perhaps the productive powers of the soil are not fully utilized under the present system of farming; so far as the small land-

---

astonished, if suddenly told that he would never get more (than his seer), for it was no uncommon thing for the manager to be deposed, and one of those holding seer to be promoted to the post."—P. 71, Unao Report.

* S., ... for instance is an immense undivided village with a rental of between Rs. 8,500 and 9,000; in the Nawabi all the co-sharers save one lived on the profits of their seer; that one managed the rest of the village, enjoyed the profits, withstood the oppressions of native officials, protected his co-sharers from all annoyance, and by his wealth and influence raised himself to almost an equality with the neighbouring noblemen. When, however, the khewat or register of shares had to be prepared the co-sharers woke up; each claimed his ancestral share; there were lengthy law-suits; at the same time the land-tax was raised nearly 100 per cent. The former well-to-do headman has ruined himself in the efforts to keep up his old style of living with a reduced income, and his co-sharers have involved themselves in debt by launching into extravagant expenditure: what with law-suits, the heavily increased land-tax, the late bad seasons, and their own mismanagement the land-owners now owe some Rs. 12,000, for which they have to pay the usual crushing interest; in a few years they will all be irretrievably ruined.

owners are concerned, a neglect to apply capital to developing the resources of their land cannot be charged against them, since they have no capital, while, so far as improvements or the growth of particular crops as market-garden produce are checked by caste prejudices, they cannot be harshly censured for reasons which have already been glanced at.*

It is true that some villages are ruined by the oppression of the tenantry, either because the landowners compel them to pay up their rents in years of agricultural distress, or because they endeavour to force up the rental by a continual enhancement of the rents; ordinary tenants are prompt to abscond if they are unduly pressed; it is chiefly the Muraus and Kurmis, the careful cultivators of the better kinds of soil, and of the most remunerative crops, who can be rack-rented at will, as they cannot afford to abandon their old thoroughly manured and laboriously prepared fields. It must be recollected that if, Government refuses to allow any remission in years of bad harvests, it can hardly expect the landowners to show much mercy towards their tenants, and the rack-renting is chiefly caused by a sudden enhancement of the Government revenue assessments, based not on actually existing but on assumed fancy rentals.

It is often represented that the embarrassments of the landed classes are in a great measure traceable to their intense love of quarrelling, and to their excessive proneness to litigation. No sufficient evidence has however yet been adduced to show that the landowner is in proportion to the necessities of his position more ready to fly to the law courts than any other classes of society; the expenditure of money in litigation is doubtless a grave additional item in

* It would not appear possible to greatly improve the husbandry of the Indian agriculturists, save in respect to a more constant supply of water by the construction of wells in outlying lands, and by securing a more plentiful stock of manure.

the burden, which landowners have now to bear, but it has yet to be shown that they seek the aid of the courts *without due cause to any considerable extent,* or that they, above all other men, are endowed with an excessive lust for wrangling. It must never be forgotten, how many various occasions arise for litiga tion in the relations which exist between Government and the landowner, between the different members of the proprietary community and between the landlord and his tenant. It is further to be recollected that under our rule violence of all kinds is a dangerous amusement, and that in the face of obstinate default by a co-sharer or a cultivator, there is no remedy save a suit in a law court.*

In the province of Oudh, where it has been found necessary to determine the title to every plot of ground in every district in conjunction with a revision of the land revenue, the occasions for and the temptation to litigation have been abnormal, and they have no doubt seriously helped to cripple the owners of landed property. The latter were called on to pay up at once a largely increased land-tax, at the very time when they were employing all their available time and all their available income in contesting innumerable claims in every law court either as plaintiff or defendant; the campaign was opened by the boundary settlement, it was followed by the field survey, and it culminated in the preparation of the judicial record of rights. The country has been flooded with troops of Amins, Munsarims, Sadr Munsarims, Chaprasis, and process-servers,† all of

* I shall not easily forget the bewildered look, which came over the face of the agent of a very wealthy native landowner, when I described to him the position and circumstances of an English squire; as one explained gradually the absence of small cultivators, the non-existence of a notice of ejectment, the extreme paucity of law-suits, the insignificant amount of the land-tax and its permanent character, he could give vent to nothing but short exclamations of utter astonishment.

† Various native officials. Amin is a surveyor; Munsarim and Sadr Munsarims help the settlement officer in the preparation of the required registers.

whom have fattened on the disturbance necessarily created by the invasion of the "Hakim Bundobust" (settlement officer), while the long contested claims and counterclaims have excited much ill-feeling between the various successful and unsuccessful litigants, an ill-feeling which has from time to time displayed itself with fatal effect in riots and other breaches of the public peace.

The most ordinary course of events in the life of a village community brings forth however quite a sufficient harvest of inevitable causes for contention, even if we quite exclude from consideration all such special reasons for litigation and quarrels, as are afforded by an official investigation into all titles in land on the annexation of a new province.

The three varieties in the constitution of these village coparcenary bodies are well known, and they need not be here described; in villages where the land is all, except the seer, held in common, it is inevitable that there should be some disputes in respect to the amount of the collections, to the village expenses, and to the profit claimed by each co-sharer; in most villages the rents of the common land are theoretically to be collected by the two or three headmen, who are supposed to act together; then the co-sharers who hold seer at low rates are generally by village custom only liable to pay rent on proof, that the rents of the common or tenant-held lands are inadequate for the complete liquidation of the Government demand; they are entitled to receive their portion of the surplus profit, and they naturally quarrel if the headmen have spent in their opinion too much money on village expenses, an item, which allows a large margin for waste.

It is very difficult for the co-sharers in undivided estates to secure their due share of the profits; if the headman is of a domineering or extravagant character, he refuses to render the yearly returns of profits and losses (samjhauta); the co-sharers must sue in the law courts, but as the village accountant is naturally the retainer of the headman, they are ignorant what their share may be, and they have constantly to file a stamp for a lump sum far in excess of the real quota due to them; it is very difficult for them under any circumstances to prove the details of their claim.

In other villages each co-sharer holds his share separately, and he knows what his quota of the revenue demand amounts to; he pays this to the lumbardar, or head of his thok, but he must be careful to see that the latter really applies the money to its proper purpose, or a month hence the Tahsildar may call on him for his portion, and he may find that the sum paid to the lumbardar has never reached the Government treasury; unfortunately also there are but few villages in which all the lands have been thus divided.

In this class of villages, however, quarrels are not frequent, and they are settled without much difficulty; it is in what are commonly known as "imperfect pattidari" (*i.e.*, partially divided) villages that the disputes between the co-sharers are the most common and the most bitter.* In these unfortunately constituted villages some portion of the cultivated area is held in common, while the village site, the unculturable waste, the small lakes and tanks, and the jungle are always so held as the undivided property of the community.

In the "undivided" villages the co-sharers are accustomed to the management of the common lands by the heads of their body, and in "completely divided" ones all the land is separately held, but in these "partially divided" estates the common lands are the subject of constant quarrels; the members of one sub-division have broken up jungle at considerable expense, and the members of another sub-division claim their share of the profit, though they have not aided in the reclamation of the waste land; one sharer wishes a tenant of his to receive the fields, another

* These are the townships described by Sir W. Maine as those "in which the community held the common mark in mixed ownership, and cultivated the arable mark in lots appropriated to the several families."—Cf. Village Communities, p. 78.

desires to till them himself; one has an old grudge against the present cultivator, and he declares he will have him ejected; the cultivator is in league with another of his many landlords, and he pays him all his rents, and the latter refuses to give up any of his unlawful gains; each sharer holds himself entitled to collect, and he exacts his share of the rent due from the unfortunate cultivator; the latter gets no receipts, and his life is a burden to him; one co-sharer wants to stack his manure on a plot of common ground, and another co-sharer refuses to allow him to do so; one seizes a scrap of the village site for a threshing-floor, and some other member of the community promptly claims his right to a portion of it; one co-sharer gathers in all the wild rice of the lake, and another forces the wild-nut (singhara) lessee to pay to him the whole of his rent.*

There is a large Mahomedan townlet which had been the ancestral joint property of respectable Syad and Sheikh community for centuries previous to the annexation of Oudh. In the Nawabi the landowners had been the Chaudhris and Kanungos of the pargana, and they were usually asked by the neighbouring landowners to become their securities with

* It is impossible to give stronger proof of the necessity of dividing the common lands, than that afforded by the Oudh Inspector-General of Police in his last annual report. Colonel Barrow writes, that regarding the causes, that principally lead to riots under these heads, he hase made careful inquiries from the much experienced of his native inspectors, several of them Oudh men, and landholders of the province, and "they give it as their opinion, that these riots for the most part arise in coparcenary villages or estates; that in many instances when the revenue courts have declared some party to have lost his right, he fights for possession with the person to whom the property has been decreed; that in these villages generally waste land, tanks, wells, groves, &c., are held in common, and are not partitioned off, though the revenue department khewat may show them as divided into shares." The heads referred to are land, tanks, crops, groves, grazing and rent, and out of 244 riots 147 are referred to these causes, but many of these referred to "other causes" are connected with land as straw, water for cattle, dividing share, right to fish in pond, right to cut grass, &c., &c.

the revenue farmer for the payment of the revenue demand; they often quarrelled among themselves, but there were no law courts for the indulgence of litigation and the disputes were usually settled by the strong hand; if the Sheikhs were defeated, the Syads received the Government engagement, and, if the Sheikhs got the upper hand, the Syads were dispossessed of the lease, but, when either the Sheikhs or the Syads lost the revenue engagement, they still retained their seer, their groves, their gardens, and their burial-places in undisturbed proprietorship.

At annexation quarrels could only be settled in the law courts; the lands were all held in common and the Sheikhs and Syads had each two lumbardars; these latter should have collected in union the rent of the common lands, and these collections should have been sufficient to pay off the Government revenue in addition to the village expenses, and a sum of 5 per cent. on the collections due to the headmen for their trouble and responsibility. The regular settlement brought an evil genius to the front; this man Musahib Ali was not one of the original proprietary body; he had only married a daughter of a Syad sharer, and through his wife he obtained a very small share in the townlet; he stirred up the Syads first to claim the whole townlet and then to fight the Sheikhs for every one of the shares; after he had thus maintained a constant succession of law-suits for nearly two years, he finally by dint of continual petitions obtained the appointment of headman, although the other members of the proprietary body appealed to the highest revenue authority in the Province.

The whole cultivated area of the townlet, with the exception of the seer, was held in common, and the four headmen were supposed to amicably collect the rents of this tenant-rented land, to jointly pay off the land-tax and to jointly divide the balance after the deduction of all expenses among themselves and their co-sharers. Directly, however, Musahib Ali was made headman, he proceeded to set at naught the principle of united action; he had extravagant and dissipated habits; he collected from the common tenants all the rent which he could force them to pay, and he spent the money on his own pleasures and expenses; the other headmen sued him year by year, but they rarely got any satisfaction; he kept a number of paid witnesses, who were ready to swear to anything and he was intimately acquainted with the procedure of the courts; the other headmen in despair applied for the complete partition of the village into separate mahals, or at least for the division of the common lands; the first request could not be sanctioned, because all the co-sharers held seer in every corner of the cultivated area, and, as some of them would not agree to an interchange of fields, the formation of separate compact estates was found to be an impossibility. There was no law allowing the Collector any power to effect imperfect partition, and the other headmen could therefore obtain no relief; Musahib Ali managed to retain his post, till in three years he had ruined himself, his own co-sharers, and the other landowners in the other three sub-divisions; in that townlet there are now but few shares in the possession of the original owners, yet there can be no doubt that, if the common lands could have been divided a few years ago, many of the co-sharers would have been saved from ruin.

There is a village, where there were year by year bitter disputes among the 20 or 30 co-sharers concerning the rents of a few acres of common rice land; each co-sharer regularly exacted from the tenant his alleged share of the rent, which would vary from an anna to six pie, till at last the cultivators were driven to despair, and the land was abandoned altogether; in the Nawabi such contentions would have been speedily settled, but, under our system of rule, there is no remedy save a costly suit.*

* Sir W. Sleeman, when speaking of some advantages which at any rate resulted from the expulsion of the smaller landholders by such

There is another village, where a whole plot of ground, amounting to 37 acres, has lain out of cultivation for eight years, because, as the co-sharers admit, they cannot agree, which of their body should be allowed to cultivate it. Innumerable instances might be given,* where the ruin of a

---

men as Rajah Darshan Singh, notes that "the greatest benefit conferred on the lands which they hold has been in the suppression of the fearful contests which used to be perpetual between the small proprietors of the military classes, among whom the lands had become minutely subdivided by the law of inheritance, about boundaries and rights to water for irrigation."—P. 164, Vol. I.

* I subjoin further instances:—

B. is an imperfect pattidari village held by a large body of Paonwars; these men were well-to-do, and they had invariably paid up the revenue with great punctuality, and no sale or mortgage of shares had yet taken place. There was, however, a patch of common jungle land on the outskirts of the village, which had lately been ploughed up without any allotment of shares by some of the pattidars; as the plot was not regularly divided, some of the co-sharers had possessed themselves of more than their due portion. Then a bitter quarrel arose respecting this land, and this hitherto peaceable community was soon divided into factions.

With great wisdom all the pattidars, with the exception of one headman, agreed to apply for a partition; they had no desire whatever for the division of the village into separate mahals (estates) but, as this was the only partition allowed by the Act, they were obliged to apply for such a division; they wished of course that each pattidar should retain his old seer fields, his hereditary groves, and his old tenant-rented land, but a field by field (khetbat) partition could not be sanctioned; then they held a council and came forward offering to agree to a complete chakbat (in blocks) division of the village, if only the Sarkar (Government) would settle their dispute; this *bête noir*, the solitary objector, obstinately refused to assent to a redistribution of his seer and tenant-rented fields; the field map showed, that his land lay in all parts of the village, and a compact partition was impossible without his consent; in spite of urgent remonstrances he resolutely refused to give way, the real fact being that he held the best of the newly ploughed-up fields, and he meant to keep them in his own possession if he could; the pattidars in despair asked the "Sarkar" at least to divide the jungle land some how or other as they felt certain that

prosperous community can distinctly be traced to the inpracticable nature of the village constitution; it is abso-

---

their intestine quarrels would ruin the village, but no help could be afforded them, and the village was abandoned to strife and litigation simply owing to the obstinacy and selfishness of one member of the proprietary body.

I know a "zamindari" (undivided) village, in which one co-sharer unable to obtain from the headman his portion of the profits, and having in vain attempted to secure a partition, sold his share (1 anna 4 pie) to an Eurasian, admittedly in order to bring into the village some "zabardast" (powerful) stranger, through whom he could be revenged on the headman of his thok (sub-division.)

There is another village in which two pattidars have every year been charged with breaches of the peace arising from their disputes in respect to the collections of the common land of the thok; one applied for partition, but it was impossible to create minute mahals, and of course the application was rejected; an hour's work could have effected imperfect partition, and would have settled the quarrel for ever.

There is another "zamindari" village for one thok of which one Dhan S. is headman. This person is a man of extravagant habits and he lives usually in another pargana; the land of his thok is all held in common except the seer; he himself rarely goes near the village, but when the harvest is ripe he despatches his son to collect and carry off all the rent; when the kists (instalments of revenue) fall due, the Tahsildar invariably finds it almost impossible to collect any revenue, and the co-sharers find it equally difficult to secure any share of the profits.

The lands of the thok cannot be divided between the co-sharers, since in the first place they lie intermixed with the lands of the other thok, and even if they could be divided field by field it would be most inexpedient to create two or three small estates, for the whole land-tax of the village only amounts to Rs. 400; a partition into compact estates is of course an impossibilty, as the co-sharers of the other thok would never consent to surrender their seer fields; of course a new headman could be appointed, but he would assuredly behave just like his predecessor; what is wanted here is a change in the constitution from "zamindari" to "pattidari;" then, if any one pattidar fails to pay his quota, he can be separately punished; as it is the "thok" is always in arrears; it is generally under attachment, and the co-sharers are involved in ruin.

lutely unsuited to our system of administration, yet as will be seen, when we come to deal with the second part of the subject, the law admits of no sufficient remedy.

In addition to the inevitable disputes between the different members of the proprietary body there are the equally unavoidable contentions between the landlords and the tenants. A landlord in England has merely to collect his rent from a small number of well-to-do farmers; a landlord in this country has to induce scores of small cultivators to pay up annually their share of the total rental. The smaller landowners are so poor, that one contested suit for the ejectment of a refractory tenant, or for the recovery of arrears of rent drives them to the money-lender, and with so many tenants it is not the owner's fault if even in small villages he is compelled every year to resort to the law courts.

T... is another "imperfect pattidari" village, which was threatened with ruin owing to a dispute between the pattidars in respect to some common jungle land. One wealthy co-sharer had with the tacit consent of the community ploughed up the land at his own expense, but, when the fields began to yield good crops, the other co-sharers claimed portions according to their ancestral shares; they quarrelled over this jungle for two or three years, and it was clear that, if it could not be divided, the community would soon be ruined. Now nothing could be done under the Act, for the co-sharers had tried that refuge, and it had failed them; they also tried to effect their object by a civil suit but the civil court had no jurisdiction. What then was to be done? At last the landowners were convinced that, if this common land was not divided, they would all be involved in common destruction, so they agreed to allow one of the district officers to divide it for them; the jungle land was then equitably distributed among the different sharers with a special allowance for the original reclaimer of this waste land, and this partition has preserved the village from costly litigation as well as from fierce intestine disputes.

It would be unreasonable, however, to expect a recurrence of such an amicable resolution; indeed I know, that these men have since fallen out respecting some other common lands, since they came and asked for a similar partition, but, as all would not agree this time, the petition was rejected.

The high rates of interest extorted by the money-lenders from all classes alike only press with exceptional severity upon the landed proprietors, because they alone are subject to a perpetual steady drain on their resources in the shape of a fiscal tax levied by the resistless hand of a strong Government. They necessarily therefore have to resort more steadily and more regularly to the usurers, than other classes of society, while, as their property is in land, their indebtedness loses to them, that which can never be recovered, namely, their ancestral estate; their inability to pay off their debt crushes them more effectually and more permanently than the inability of a man, who has merely moveables wherewith to satisfy his creditor.

The landowner, on whose lands not an encumbrance exists, is compelled to pay the same high rate as the cultivator who possesses nothing but his crop and his plough bullocks; on the one side is a strong guild of grasping money-lenders, and on the other side is an ignorant rustic; even if the latter had sufficient intelligence and determination to resist the excessive demand of the money-lender, it is doubtful if he would prevail in the struggle; liable every year to a steady drain on his resources, and directed by Government Officers to pay up the revenue tax at fixed dates, and in fixed instalments his need for ready money, even if his estate be quite free from liens, is very frequent and very pressing; the money can be so easily secured by agreeing to the terms offered, and it may possibly not be obtained at all, or at any rate not in sufficient time, if he holds out for higher interest. With the want of foresight and intelligence, which as yet characteriz[illegible]atives, he prefers to satisfy the Government demand, and to leave his future prospects to take care of themselves.

He borrows a hundred rupees, and in three years he finds that he has not paid much of the heavy interest, that the balance at compound interest has swelled to Rs. 200; he is threatened with a law-suit; he blindly signs a fresh bond for the whole sum claimed, of which one-half only represents the principal, and in this new bond he is probably compelled to mortg age his property, to give up possession to the money-lender, who is to receive the profits in lieu of interest, and it is doubtless stipulated, that, if at the end of the fixed term, the principal is not repaid, the mortgage is to become a sale; once well in the money-lender's grip the landowner has small chance of escape.

The relations which existed between the money-lender and the landowner under the Native Government have quite demoralized the latter; every landowner had in those days, as now, a permanent running account with the local money-lender; complete liquidation was never contemplated by either party, nor did the money-lender obtain full payment of his interest; he was satisfied, if, on the whole, he received sufficient remuneration; neither party then proceeded to extremities; if the money-lender became too stingy, he lost his customer, while if the landowner used his *lathi* (club), he lost his money bags. Under our rule the money-lender has gained a friend in our civil courts, while the landowner has lost the free use of his only help, the bamboo club.

There is a large Syad village, which the landowners pressed by sudden necessity mortgaged nominally for Rs. 10,000 to a city banker. This 10,000 did not all represent principal, for much of it was old debt, nor had the principal been all received by the owners; the mortgagor was to hold possession for ten years, and the profits were only to be applied to payment of the interest. At the end of ten years the mortgage becomes a sale, if the owners cannot pay off the sum named in the bond; the yearly rental of that village was at the time of the mortgage about Rs. 10,000, and the money-lender will assuredly obtain the ownership for the loan of a sum which only represents one year's rental, and this is a fair type of most transactions of the kind.*

* It must not be supposed that the services rendered by the money-lending village banians are overlooked; they are in many districts the

The money-lenders are only too ready to supply loans to any landowners; they merely stipulate for a rate of interest, which they know will sooner or later bring the borrower's property into their grasp; the necessity of the latter coupled with his want of prudent foresight leads him blindly into the meshes; borrowing is so easy, and for the time so pleasant a mode of satisfying other pressing liabilities; a few years hence, and he gnashes his teeth in impotent despair, while the money-lender draws in the net.

There is unfortunately but little capital in the possession of the landed classes; it is not possible for them to borrow at reasonable interest in order to expend money on the improvement of their estates; the landowners as a body are in the power of the money-lenders, who grow sleek and fat on usury, for "it is the canker and ruine of many men's estates which in processe of time breeds a publike povertie."

The State claims its right to half the landowner's rental, but while it thus exacts 50 per cent. of the latter's supposed annual collections, it gives him small aid towards their realization; it does, it is true, establish courts, in which he can sue for the recovery of unpaid rent, but, before he can obtain a decree, or at any rate long before he has been able

---

main stay of revenue and rent collection, but they do bleed their well-to-do rustic and reckless customers with the same measure, that they mete out to insolvent debtors.

The Unao settlement officer notes, that "in the Nawabi ordinary money-lenders were very chary about advancing loans on security of landed property, and consequently money was not easily obtained; further the system of demanding security, before allowing a man to engage for his village contributed greatly to keep down extravagance, the security being always on the watch to see, that the village collections were not misapplied, whereas now money-lenders are only too glad to advance any sum that may be required; indeed I know men, who have sent out agents to prompt the zamindars to borrow of them, and the security system being done away with, every one doeth that which seems good in his own eyes unchecked and unwarned."—Unao Report, para. 96.

to realize that decree, he has been obliged to pay up the full Government demand;* for instance, his assumed rental is Rs. 500 and his land-tax amounts to Rs. 250; the crops fail, and some of the tenants have to spend their rents in marrying their daughters, and he can only collect Rs 400, of which he of course pays Rs. 200 to the treasury. To obtain the other Rs. 100 of which 50 are due to the State as land-revenue, he sues in the rent courts; he must file a stamp costing Rs. 7-6, besides fees for the summoning of the various defaulting tenants calculated at 6 annas for each summons; he will probably have to call witnesses, some of whom must be summoned, and provided also with money for the expenses of the journey to and from the court; the village accountant will similarly have to be sent for and fed; perhaps one or two of the defendants fail to appear, and a warrant, costing one rupee, is issued for their arrest; probably a native pleader will have to be called in, and then his fees, and the costs of a power of attorney will swell the amount of costs; the native clerk of the court, and the judge's orderly will receive doubtless a small present; when he obtains a decree, he will then have to expend about Rs. 2 in obtaining a copy; on obtaining a copy he will have to file a petition on stamped paper for execution; this will require further a statement of the goods of the judgment-debtor, which he may desire to have attached. All these petitions cost money, since they are written in the Persian character by some copyist who squats under the trees outside the court. The costs of the issue of a warrant of

* So in Lower Bengal Mr. Mill in his History of British India, Vol. V., p. 367, notices, that "a cause which accelerated, but by no means produced the ruin of the zamindars (for the incompatibility of their characters with the situation, in which they were placed, led infallibly to the same result), was the delay which they experienced in obtaining payment from the ryots. The Government had given to themselves the benefit of summary process with regard to the zamindars. But they left the zamindars to the tedious progress through all the technical forms of the Courts in extracting payment from the ryots. The Collector of Burdwan, who stated the matter correctly in reporting to

arrest or for attachment must be paid in. At last off go the decree-holder, and the process-server to seize the goods of the judgment-debtor; when they arrive at the house, however, it is found, that the unlucky decree-holder, being unable to enter his tenant's dwelling-house, in order to find out what articles of property the latter may possess, has given an incorrect inventory; in many cases the tenant has long ago concealed, or removed away his valuables, and the process-server, after attaching a brasspot and a charpoy (wooden bedstead) which at any rate are certain "finds" in a peasant's house, returns to the court with perhaps six penny's worth of articles. Before the plaintiff can obtain further notice of his outstanding decree, he will have to once more file petitions with a fresh inventory, and, even if he succeeds in realizing the sum decreed, it is not probable, that the tenant will be able to pay the costs of the suit; it is no use to sell the latter's plough or bullocks, even were such a sale legal, since the tenant would then abandon his holding, and the other cattle have long ago been handed over by the debtor to some relative or friend for safe custody, till the danger has passed. The landlord has thus been forced to pay the cost of suing for the Government share of the rent due, as well as his own portion; he has probably been obliged to borrow at heavy interest to pay off the Rs. 50 balance of the land-tax, in

---

Government the following complaint of the Rajah 'who submits it,' he says, to your consideration, 'whether or no it can be possible for him to discharge his duties to Government, with that punctuality which the Regulations require, unless he be armed with powers as prompt to enforce payment from his renters, as Government has been pleased to authorize the use of, in regard to its claims on him; and he seems to think, it must have proceeded from an oversight, rather than from any just and avowed principle, that there should have been established two modes of judicial process under the same Government; the one summary, and efficient for the satisfaction of its own claims; the other tardy and uncertain in regard to the satisfaction of the claims due to its subjects; more especially in a case like the present, where ability to discharge the one demand necessarily depends on the other demand being previously realized.'"

addition to the costs of the suit and even in the end he may regard himself as fortunate, if he secure payment of the sum decreed, *minus* the costs of this litigation; in many instances he barely realizes the costs.*

The whole cost of litigation and the whole expenses of collection are thrown upon the landowner, and it must be recollected that the legal expenses are a new item in the burdens of landed property. There were no rent courts and no Civil Procedure Codes under the native Governments to increase the embarrassments of the proprietors of land; if a tenant could pay in those days he was forced to do so without delay, or else his house was burnt down, and he himself driven out of the village; he could not pay his debts, or marry his daughters with the produce of his field, and then laugh at the ineffectual efforts of the landowner to recover the unpaid rent through the agency of a law-suit; he has little to lose by a decree, for, if the landowner eject him, he will lease a few outlying fields of a neighbouring village, and keep his bullocks in his new landlord's yard.

It will be asked why the landowner does not proceed to distrain the crop of the defaulting tenant, if the procedure by a law-suit bears such poor fruit. It must be recollected, however, that the low caste tenants, as a rule, pay their rent punctually, and that it is the under-proprietor, the holder of seer land, or the sharer in a sub-settled village, who is the usual defaulter. The Oudh Rent Act does not allow the crops of an under-proprietor, that is a sub-holder, who has secured a heritable and transferable right on his land, to come under the operation of the distress law; the landowner has no

* Notwithstanding every effort the Oudh rent courts only succeeded in obtaining full satisfaction of decrees in 41 per cent. out of 13,490 decrees passed in 1873, and in 42 per cent. out of 12,047 decrees passed in 1874: in those years respectively 2,203 and 1,841 decrees were partially executed, and in 4,567 and 4,195 cases there was no execution.—Report of Judicial Commissioner, 1874, p. 74.

option therefore; the law only gives him one remedy, and that is but a broken reed; as the manager of a large estate said, "neither do you allow us to collect the rents from these men in our own way, nor do you aid us to collect them in your way." The Oudh under-proprietor, secure therefore from all fear of distraint, cuts, reaps, stores, eats and sells his crop, long before the decree is given against him, even if the landowner cares to prosecute his claim by resorting to this costly remedy; when once the produce of the field is gone beyond recovery, it is useless for the land-owner to seek for payment through the law courts.*

The same difficulty is experienced in a still greater degree, when the case is one of default by a whole village; a bad season comes, the cattle have died of murrain, or the frost has killed the ripening spring crops, and the under-proprietors refuse to pay a penny; the Collector of course presses the proprietor to pay the land-tax; he borrows the required sum and clears off the balance; he then sues with heavy initial expenses to recover the arrears due from the under-proprietary community; he obtains his decree and he applies for sale, but the courts refuse to sell, deeming that a temporary attachment will suffice to pay off the decrees; the village is attached and placed in the Collector's charge under Section 125 of the Rent Act;† the Collector has of course no time to superintend the management, and not

* As is noted in the Oudh Revenue Report "at present the landowner has no means of realizing his dues from a recusant under-proprietor, but to sue him for his arrears and the process is found to be cumbrous, costly, and ineffectual."

And again on p. 91 of Revenue Report for 1872, it is observed, that "the only machinery provided by the Rent Act for the realization of rent from defaulting under-proprietors is slow and cumbrous in the extreme, and experience has convinced the Chief Commissioner that in the interests of the superior and inferior owners alike, a swifter and simpler means of calling the under-proprietor to account must be introduced."

† "Both in the collection of rents, and in the liquidation of debts, a large measure of success might fairly have been expected, and in a con-

even the current rents are collected; so matters go on from bad to worse; the proprietor is indeed relieved of the liability to pay the revenue, but he has lost his small share of the profit, and his income is somewhat reduced; the under-proprietors become demoralized; they quarrel and wrangle with the Government manager; the tenants pay their rents secretly to the under-proprietors, and the under-proprietors refuse to pay anything to anybody; they let their fields fall out of cultivation, and the attachment of their crops yields little; in short, the village quickly becomes a ruin.* The authorities naturally hesitate to sanction sale because they dislike to eject the ancestral holders; the debt meanwhile increases, the Government revenue even is not realized, and the costs of management is barely defrayed.

Under the native administration the Rajah, in order to force his sub-holders to pay, could make use of all the coercive processes which the revenue collector could employ against the defaulting independent landowner; he could arrest the defaulter, imprison him in his fort and send his agent with a body of retainers to collect the rents due from the cultivators; he could attach and carry off the under-pro-

---

siderable number of cases it is evident that the management has failed in the object with which it was or should have been undertaken by the liquidation of the debt *within a reasonable period.* District officers have hitherto been too much in the habit of undertaking, as a matter of course, the management of an estate attached in execution of a decree without first ascertaining whether the condition of the estate was such that the debts could by such an arrangement be liquidated within a reasonable time, and that therefore the attempt might be made in the interests of the judgment-debtor without inflicting undue hardships on the decree-holder, who had applied for the sale of the property."—Cf. para. 28, Oudh Revenue Report, 1874.

* Sometimes even the under-proprietors secretly set fire to the crops when they have been attached, or induce some of the village laborers to steal the grain from the threshing-floor, or in the face of the Government manager they defiantly carry off the produce of their fields; it would require a band of policemen with muskets to prevent some of these desperate men from laying their hands on their own crops.

prietor's wheat and sugarcane; he could drive him off to the jungle, plunder and burn down his house, seize his moveable property, and even sell his wife and children, or if he could catch the fugitive, he could torture him and force him to sell or transfer his share to some other solvent kinsman. There were then no accumulating arrears; before the coming year's arrangements were made, all dues had to be paid up, or remitted in due course by the landlord. In those days too a great many of the under-proprietary body served with the Rajahs as their retainers and fightingmen; each Hindu chieftain maintained a large force of such dependents in his fort to assist him in his struggles against the Nazims of the day; they were supported from the surplus revenues of the estate, for few of the landowners could be forced in the latter days of the native administration to pay more than a third or even a smaller portion of their actual rental to the State.* A large number of the under-proprietary body served in the army, and their remittances helped their kinsmen to defray the Rajah's demand; the few residents could therefore in those days afford to pay even two-thirds of the rental to the chief. Now however with the continuous increase in the number of the resident co-sharers, there is scarcely enough for the subsistence of their families in the scanty pittance, which remains to each sharer, after the liquidation of the Talukdar's decreed rent and of the village expenses.

They, like the independent landowners, paid in many cases their quota towards the expenses of the revenue survey, and of the demarcation of boundaries; they had to expend large sums in their struggle against the Talukdar

---

* Sir W. Sleeman observes, that "generally in Oudh, the larger landholders do not pay more than one-third of their net rents to the Government, while some of them do not pay one-fifth, or one-tenth. In the half of the territory made over to us in 1801, the great landholders, who still retain their estates, pay to our Government at least two-thirds of their net rents."

in the law courts, before they could obtain their decree for sub-settlement; they entered into possession therefore saddled with heavy old debts, and, just at the very time, when they were most unable to manage their estate properly, just when a little ready money was urgently required to start them on their struggle, the largely enhanced revenue demand greatly increased their payments, and a series of disastrous harvests, floods, murrain, drought, frost, and hail crushed them to the ground, and rendered the prospect of their recovery well nigh hopeless.

Whereas before the annexation many of these under-proprietors lived on the best of terms with the superior proprietor and regarded their interests, and those of the latter as identical, the summary settlement of 1856, which ejected the Talukdars and restored the under-proprietor to the independent possession of his village sowed the seeds of animosity;* in 1858 the tables were turned, and the Talukdar recovered possession. The feelings of hatred between many of the old proprietors and the Talukdar have been intensified by protracted litigation in the settlement courts; those who have obtained decrees for sub-settlement are conspicuous defaulters, and those who have been unsuccessful are equally resolved not to pay more rent to the Talukdar than the State can compel them to contribute; the Talukdar strives to ruin them, and they in their turn yearn to see their antagonist reduced to the same straits, as those to which they themselves have been reduced through his agency, and the policy of our Government.

---

* During the mutiny many of the Talukdars revenged themselves on the under-proprietors by an indiscriminate plunder of the villages; even those birtias who had acquired their rights originally from the superior owner, and had always held in subordination to him, received from us the independent possession of their villages, and the large proprietors naturally endeavoured during the anarchy of 1857 to wreak their revenge on these under-proprietors by burning their houses, goods, and title-deeds, and by destroying all proofs of their rights, which might be in existence.

PART II.

PROPOSED REMEDIES.

CHAPTER IV.

CHANGES REQUIRED IN OUR SYSTEM OF ASSESSMENT.

Portia.—" Then must the Jew be merciful."

An attempt has been made to set forth, with as much clearness as possible, the various causes which have contributed, and are still contributing daily to this steady transfer of hereditary landed property from the hands of the original owners to strangers, and to establish the conclusion that Government was not entirely free from the charges of having by its ill-advised system of administration added to the embarrassments and of having consequently hastened on the ruin of the hereditary proprietors.

The evil is admittedly a serious one, and various remedies have been proposed in different quarters. The Government of the North-West Provinces has taken a prominent part in the discussion of this question, but it has apparently confined its endeavours to securing the land-owners, *when dispossessed,* certain privileges as tenants in the shape of fixed favorable rents. In the Punjab inquiries have been made in regard to the extent of these transfers of landed property, but the statistics collected, although, in the opinion of Sir Henry Davis, they tend to show, that the supposed number of these alienations has been over-estimated by some officers, do not seem thoroughly reliable.

The Chief Commissioner of the Central Provinces (Mr. Morris) has, it seems, submitted some proposals to the Government of India, but their nature has not been divulged. Sir George Couper has in forcible language stated his own views of the situation, and his remarks deserve careful attention.* An endeavour will now be made to

* P. 45., Oudh Revenue Report, 1873.

"The Chief Commissioner is however quite satisfied of one thing, and it is this :—It is a question which admits of no tinkering. It is no

grapple with the difficult question of remedial measures and to suggest, if possible, some changes in our system of rule, which would, it is hoped, in some degree check this constant transfer of estates and render the circumstances of the landowners of these provinces more enviable than unfortunately they can now be considered.

---

use lifting up our hands in horror and dismay and calling for reports, and uttering platitudes about the land passing out of the hands of the ancient race. We must either accept the situation, or alter our system of government altogether, for it is that system which has called this state of things into existence and is perpetuating it. It is owing to our system that the thousands, who formerly aided the soil with their earnings sent from afar, are now living on it a dead burden, where they were formerly an active support. It is owing to our system that girls are reared in hundreds, not only to be so many more mouths to feed, but to involve their fathers in still deeper debt to meet their marriage expenses. It is owing to our system that men are no longer allowed to kill each other by scores in agrarian quarrels, that the march of famine and epidemic disease is checked, that quinine is being brought to the door of every fever-stricken sufferer, and that in every district there are sanitary measures in progress, which have for their object the mitigation of disease, and the prevention of death. Owing to the operation of all these causes, the population which have only the land to look to for their support are annually becoming more and more numerous. The consequences are not difficult to foresee; when the land cannot yield more than is sufficient for the mouths dependent on its produce, it follows that there is nothing left wherewith to meet the demands of the State, which claims one-half of the rental, or any other demand."

"Consequently, from whatever quarter the demand is made, the people are unable to meet it, and the land which is the security for the claim must be transferred in satisfaction of what is due upon it."

"Such the Chief Commissioner repeats, is the inevitable result of the present system of administration, so long as the people adhere to their old habits and prejudices, so long as they put no sort of restraint on the indulgence of their several instincts, so long as they consider it creditable to ruin themselves on the expenses of a daughter's marriage, so long in short as the leopard does not change his spots. It is the business of higher authority to determine whether the blessings of our rule counterbalance its disadvantages. But it is certain we cannot give a country all the benefit of civilization and allow the dwellers therein at the same time those advantages which they derived from being in a state of semi-barbarism."

The subject naturally divides itself into two parts, and it will be convenient first to consider some suggestions for the amendment of our present methods of assessment and then to bring forward some proposals for the improvement of our system of collection.

The nature of some of the required remedies has been already adverted to. There can be no reasonable doubt that the land-tax has of late years in Oudh and in the North-West Provinces not only been raised suddenly 50 and 100 per cent., but that the enhanced demand in many districts in these administrations has been fixed at sums, which did at the time of the imposition of the revised land-tax, and may still represent far more than the real half of the rent-roll.*

The injustice of a system of assessment, which *pretaxes* the landowners in expectation of a future increase in their rentals, either from their own exertions, or from natural causes, is self-evident; for the future, strict orders should be given that assessors are to base their assessments on the actual assets of estates, and that, if in particular cases it should appear on thoroughly reliable grounds, that the rental will in the course of a few years be greatly increased from the operation of any well-defined causes, the Government share of that estimated increase should not be collected until it is calculated that such rise will actually take place;† in

---

* Sir George Couper has, as already described, taken measures to secure an equitable adjustment of the land-tax for the province of Oudh by a systematic revision of the assessments of most of the districts.

† As a rule, it is very dangerous to speculate on a prospective increase. The data at hand are usually quite insufficient to enable the settlement officer to make an accurate forecast, except in the case, where a village has owing to some special cause deteriorated, and where it may be expected that the new fallow will be reploughed in the course of a few years.

short the tax being in fact a tax on income should be calculated on actual receipts, and not on fancy figures, or plausible contingencies. At present our land-tax is nothing but an exceedingly unjust and unequal income-tax; many of the objections raised against the income-tax can be urged with double and treble force against our present system of land revenue assessment. It is unequal in its incidence, and its collection is made at inconvenient seasons, while its assessment necessitates the expenditure of vast sums, and entails lengthy and harassing inquiries respecting the incomes and profits of the classes who bear its burden.

As already urged, the assessment must be based on facts, and not on fancies; if the landowner is not to blame for the inferior productiveness of his lands, if his rents are low from causes manifestly beyond his control, he is equitably entitled to consideration. In assessing such estates on actuals, we only return to the system so much belauded by later writers, and collect the Government share of the actual rental of the land.

Wherever the rents are wholly or partially paid in grain, wherever there are Brahman and Thakur cultivators paying at high-caste rates,* wherever there is a paucity of hardworking low-caste tenants, wherever there are herds

---

In 1822, the N.-W. P. Board of Revenue set their faces against the system of rasidi jamas, *i.e.*, a demand rising progressively according to an estimate of prospective improvement, and Mr. Holt Mackenzie approved this policy, since in his opinion such estimates had been "found to be constantly fallacious, for the increased demand frequently operated to prevent the very improvement in contemplation of which it was imposed."

* It would be well if Mr. Holt Mackenzie's observations on this point were studied. Speaking of the lower rents paid by these high-caste cultivators, he says:—"The higher castes, whose females do not assist their labors, require perhaps absolutely some such indulgence in

of wild animals, which devour the ripening crops, wherever there are lands liable to perpetual floods or drought, the assessor should be directed to assess the estates at their actual paying value, and not on fancy estimates of the extent to which their rental *might* under other circumstances be swelled. It must be clearly remembered that the test of a fair assessment is that the land-tax does represent the half of that sum, which the landowner can with ordinary diligence *collect* on the average from the estate, and not the half of an airy rack-rental, which the assessor in the calm retreats of his office may placidly evolve from his fertile and arithmetical, but exceedingly unagricultural, brain.

In regard to fallow lands, and to those fields which are not regularly tilled, it is suggested that, at the time of assessment, the settlement officer should, by a comparison of the rent-rolls for the last ten or eight years, calculate the average area of unploughed ground during that period, and he might then exempt from assessment that number of acres which, in his opinion, might henceforth be

---

almost all kinds of tillage; and their prejudices also are against their undertaking to raise the more profitable crops, which require irrigation, manure, and laborious weeding. Even indeed without any such prejudices they could not, unassisted by the labor of their families, compete with the other, and more industrious classes in raising crops requiring much care, and many hands. Nothing, I conceive, would be less humane or worse than to attempt suddenly to place all classes on a footing, and to look to the land merely, and not to the cultivator, in adjusting the public demand."—Revenue Records, N.-W. P., 1822—33, pp. 180-181.

Sir George Couper has disallowed all progressive jamas of this kind for Oudh. On p. 8, Revenue Report, 1874, it is stated that "in Kheri, Bharaich, and other districts, the progressive jama based on an anticipated future rise on rents, or on other considerations, which the settlement officer considered it right to take into account, have been disallowed, and the revised assessment will in all cases be fixed on the rental, which each estate would yield were the rents actually prevailing for similar land in the neighbourhood imposed."

expected to be tilled in an average season; the profits of any extra cultivation at a time of any unusual agricultural prosperity would form a slight set-off to the ordinary losses of husbandry in this country-losses which being of no exceptional severity would not entitle him to any relief or consideration from the State. We must either allow the landholders some slight margin of profits above the half-assets, in order to secure to them some reserve fund for the liquidation of the land-tax in years of agricultural disaster, or we must retax our rigid system of collection.

In the Partabgarh district the settlement officer (Mr. King) "save in very exceptional instances," deliberately forebore to assess the mahwah trees, for he regarded them "as a considerable resource in bad years and other times upon which the malguzar can fall back." Every village was assessed on its actual rental, and the Oudh revenue reports show that Partabgarh is the only Oudh district in which the land-tax was completely collected last year, yet the rise on the whole district was 36 per cent., and one among the few districts, where no revision of assessment has been considered necessary, and where there had been no remissions of revenue.

Probably the assessment of this district, based as it was on the rent-roll, though criticized by some as unscientific, will be hereafter recognized as one of the most successful, reliable, and equitable revisions of the land-tax in all North-West India.

It is difficult to conceive any project more disastrous than this idea of fixing a suitable land-tax by "discounting the coming rise of rent." An assessor, however great his talents, must indeed be a heaven-sent genius, if he can, after a residence of even twelve or fifteen years in India, without the slightest farming experience, without ever having grown a single crop of wheat or rice, undertake gravely to predict that in a particular district the rents will rise 20 or 30 per cent. in the course of a few years, so as to justify the immediate imposition of a tax calculated on the half of that sum to which he assumes the rental will amount at the end of the calculated interval. An assessor too may make a grave mistake, who can deliberately raise the revenue demand 50 or 100 per cent., because he considers that the rent should have risen to this extent since the imposition of the tax thirty years ago. However elaborate his calculations may be, is not this a most dangerous and apparently sound policy? Even the most experienced land-surveyor in England would shrink appalled from such a process, for it means the enhancement of the rent of thousands of small tenants, who are, on the *ipse dixit* of the assessing officer, to be reduced without mercy to destitution and beggary.

It is to be feared that numbers of that vast jail population which has flooded the prisons of Upper India during the past few years, have owed their incarceration to an excessive rack-renting, which inevitably followed the introduction of this enhanced land-tax, and that many cultivators and landowners have been reduced to great distress by a too sudden reduction of their standard of comfort.

The power given to the settlement officer for good and evil is incalculable, and it is most difficult to check him in his airy flights, if he is obstinately determined on viewing the world through the medium of rose-water; on him should be impressed by Commissioners and Boards of Revenue the well-known lines,

> Oh it is excellent
> To have a giants' strength; but it is
> Tyrannous to use it like a giant.

There can be no doubt that the landowners would, like Lucio, heartily chorus "that's well said" to any such wise admonition.

When, again, the proprietary body is very numerous, or very poor, or where the estate of a large landowner, as those of the Rajahs of Bamnipair and Manikapur already instanced, is eaten up with a numerous and struggling body of under-proprietors, living from hand to mouth, many of them with scarce a rag to cover their bodies, or a husk to eat, then in common mercy, in common humanity, the assessment must be fixed at a lower figure than would be assumed for the estate of a well-to-do single owner. Under these peculiar tenures, the sub-holder's income depends directly upon the assessment, for they have to pay to their landholder either nine-tenths or three-fourths of the estimated rental.

Where, owing to the excessive lightness of the previous assessment, the increase in the tax must necessarily be heavy, a general system of gradual enhancements is earnestly recommended.* It is as absurd as it is unjust to expect that the landed proprietors of this country will ever be able to pay suddenly a heavy rise of 50 or 100 per cent. on their assessments, or what is the same thing, that they can in a single year so alter their standard of comfort, as to feel without much suffering the sudden diminution of their income by one-half or more; it would not be fair to other landowners or to the State to let them off altogether, and, were this done, the same difficulty would come to the front in a more formidable shape at the next settlement, but it is strongly urged that on ordinary principles of fair play the

* The last Oudh Revenue Report (1874) records that "the settlement officers (in Kheri, &c.) have been told that in all cases, where the revised jama, though based on a fair estimate of the present rental, gives a large increase on the former demand, the full revised jama need not be imposed at once, but may be introduced gradually by yearly assessments spread in periods of from three to seven years, according to the amount of the inrcrease on the old demand."—P. 8, 1873.

In the North-West Provinces the new assessment is collected within six months of its announcement (cf. Messrs. Crosthwaite's edition of North-West Provinces Revenue Act, Note to Section 46). I do not know whether any gradual enhancement has been sanctioned; any how no distinct orders for general guidance in all cases have been issued by either Government; what is required is the issue of an order, that in no case shall the assessment be raised *at once* beyond a certain percentage.

State should allow them a short respite, before it calls upon them to pay up the whole of the revised demand; otherwise our system has deliberately allowed them to raise their standard of living; and, when they have been encouraged for thirty years to increase and multiply, we sternly bid them to abruptly amend their ways, and to sink to a lower level of existence; it is unreasonable to suppose that the landed classes of any country in the world could prosper under this system of assessment. If we maintain our system of thirty years' assessment, we must show more consideration for the weaknesses of poor humanity than we do at present.*

> S.—Is it so nominated in the bond?
> P.—It is not so expressed; but what of that?
> 'Twere good to do so much for charity.

---

* Mr. Bird, writing in 1832, records that "where a very great increase of revenue is obtainable, for instance, four or five times the amount of the jama previously demanded, the most liberal allowances should be made to the zamindars so as not to reduce them at a stroke from great affluence to narrow circumstances."—Selection, North-West Provinces Revenue Records, pp. 462-63. Mr. Holt Mackenzie also wrote in 1826 that he cordially concurred with the Board in desiring to secure the zamindars from the evils of a rapidly enhanced assessment.

So the Court of Directors in 1822 recorded a minute in the same sense, and the Governor-General wrote that "even where the means of raising the revenue are more abundant, where the strict right of Government to demand an increase is undoubted, and the ultimate enforcement of such a demand may be of clear expediency, they have urged the necessity of avoiding any sudden enhancement. The existing appropriation by individuals or classes of the net rent of the country may be abusive and useless, but it may not be the less inconsistent with humanity and policy for the Government to destroy, by a sudden resumption of its rights, institutions, and habits which have grown out of the relinquishment."—Revenue Records, N.-W. P., 1822—33, Allahabad, 1872.

But these wise counsels have been systematically disregarded.

It is of course useless to discuss the advantages and disadvantages of a thirty years' settlement, as the period cannot now be altered, till the revised settlements expire; it is clear also that under the present expensive and dilatory system of assessment it would be impossible to give a shorter period.

It is a mistake to suppose that even in the mere account of receipts and balances the State is a gainer in the long run by such rigorous assessments. The Oudh Revenue Reports show clearly that the introduction of a heavy land-tax will sooner or later necessitate the remission of large sums on account of uncollected assessments; first come heavy arrears of revenue with reports of extensive transfers of landed property; then follow inquiries, unrest and discontent, coupled with large remissions and suspensions resulting probably in the demoralization of the tax-payers. The Government, when too late, admits its errors; but though it be then generous and liberal, its measures of relief arrive too slowly to save many landowners from ruin, and, before these landowners have sold or mortgaged away their ancestral estates, they in their turn have played the Jew to their miserable and starving tenantry; as in Oudh so in Jhansi; you cannot suck an orange dry, and yet expect it to burst with juice.

Mr. Colvin proposes* that in future the assessing officers shall fix the rents as well as the land-tax, and that the

* Cf. A. Colvin, p. 136. Memo. on Revision of Settlements:—"The minimum of advantage with the maximum of irritation is what our so-called "competition" rents of to-day will bring us to. The remedy certainly does not lie in merely enhancing the revenue on the landlords, but I believe in recognizing the historical aspect of these so-called rents. The remedy will be found in arranging at time of settlement for the fair and full valuation of rents, not by law courts, and vain *formulæ* of enhancement, but by the only officer competent to do it. The settlement officer who stands in the place of Akbar's Amil and who has to guide him a mass of *data*, which he can only affectively handle. During the term of settlement the rents so fixed, I would with certain exceptions maintain; a far larger revenue would be gained with a smaller amount of heart-burning. The treasury would be satisfied, and the people more content."

It is almost certain, however, that Akbar's Amil did not fix the rents of the cultivators; he merely estimated the gross produce (nikasi) of each estate, and then required the village proprietary bodies to pay up that estimated rental *minus* their nankar allowances, leaving the proprietors to settle all question of rent with their cultivators.

rents thus fixed shall be maintained with certain exceptions till the next settlement. There can be no question that an assessment on rents thus fixed by the settlement officer would lighten the burdens of the landowner; he could no longer be compelled to pay up a largely .enhanced land-tax, before he had been allowed time to rack-rent his tenants.

The objections, however, to a proposal of this kind, seem very cogent. It would be possible perhaps to fix the rental, if the rents actually paid by the tenants at the time of settlement, as recorded in the rent-rolls and admitted by both cultivators and landlords to be correct, are accepted as the basis of rent-assessment,* and the tenants would be

Nothing can be further from the truth, than to assert as has been done in the official report presented to Parliament in 1871-72, that Akbar recognized no property in land. There can be no doubt that in Oudh all the various Rajput clans and chiefs retained possession of their ancestral estates in the reign of that monarch, and that Todar Mal, his great finance minister, settled the land-tax with the landholders; no attempt was made to fix the rents for the holdings of the cultivators; Todar Mal's system was exactly that followed by our settlement officers in grain-rented districts. He calculated the gross produce of the cultivated area, as sub-divided into different classes of soil, and he required the landholder to pay in cash the estimated money-value of the Government share, or, if they preferred, the fixed share of the total estimated produce. In Akbar's reign, the then Rajah of Bulrampur paid, I believe, a revenue of Rs. 5,000. The landholder was allowed to collect what he could, or what he chose from the tillers of the soil.

* Mr. Fane (Joint-Member of the Board of Revenue with Mr. Bird) expressed his decided opinion against a thirty years' fixation of rents. After recording that such a measure was neither lawful nor desirable, as it would create rights on land, where none such had previously existed, and would further prove only a half and half measure, leaving the landowner in a very anomalous position, he proceeds to point out that the scheme was also impracticable, *viz.*:—"I am of opinion that fixing the rent which each ryot shall pay to his landlord is not practicable, except at a certain loss of revenue, a large expenditure of money, and an enormous waste of time. It seems to me preposterous to suppose that Government officers can persuade ryots to pay rents, at all approaching those, they may be made and fairly

only too glad to secure immunity from fresh taxation for a period of thirty years. It would be necessary to fix the rent not merely for each cultivator's holding but for each field in that holding, inasmuch as the tenants would from time to time abandon some fields, or increase their cultivation by taking plots formerly held by others. If then the rent of each plot is not fixed, and duly recorded in the rent-roll, no transfers of fields from one cultivator to another could take place without great difficulty and considerable perplexity in respect to future payments. The process of fixing a thirty years' rent for every field throughout a large district would probably render the duration of the settlement operations twice as lengthy and tedious an undertaking as it now is; in villages, where the tenants only pay at a fixed rate on the total number of acres in their lease, the process would be one of pure speculation. At the end of these thirty years, however, it would be necessary for the assessing officers to discover not the existing rents as at present, but to what extent the rents fixed thirty years ago are now adequate or inadequate; if the assessor now finds it is difficult to determine what are the prevailing rents, it is obvious that his difficulties will be almost insuperable when he is directed to ascertain whether the rents can bear an enhancement of 15, 20, 30, 88 or 129 per cent.

As the rents have been compulsorily fixed since last settlement, he will have scarcely any reliable guides for his information. It will be necessary to estimate accurately the value of produce, the relative outturn of crops, the profits of the cultivators, the rise in prices, and the cost of cultivation. The unfortunate officer would again have to follow the procedure so strongly condemned by Mr. Colvin in the earlier pages of his note; he would be obliged to play the part of a trained land-valuer, well knowing that

made to pay by proprietors. That enormous expense and delay will attend operations, conducted on this principle, experience has already sufficiently evinced."—P. 465, N.-W. P. Revenue Selections, Allahabad, 1872.

he possessed none of the special education, or of the special agricultural knowledge required. Neither civilians nor military officers in civil employ could be trusted to make the assessment; it would be necessary to import and to maintain a separate staff of specially trained land-surveyors.*

The settlement would again "rest on a calculation of the gross produce, the cost of irrigation, and the net yield of every field;" the settlement officers would again be supposed "capable of fixing a proper rent for every field;" the productive powers of the land and the calculations of average outturn would once more become the basis of assessment in opposition to the principle warmly approved by Mr. Colvin that "the real basis of all assessments is the acknowledged rent which the land can afford to pay;" and that acknowledged rent is manifestly in most cases the recorded rental. At present the assessors have merely to discover what the prevailing rents are, and they only require that amount of agricultural knowledge, which will enable them to detect particular attempts to deceive. We should, under Mr. Colvin's system, inevitably again have the pleasing spectacle of a settlement officer spending eleven years in assessing 396 villages,† for "during eleven years in no one district had more than 396 villages been assessed."

---

* Under this system of assessment, the Collector of Balasore reported in 1829 that in his opinion the settlement of one mahal, the jama of which was only Rs. 13,586, would occupy his exclusive attention for three years during a period of three months in each year.

† Mr. Colvin's Memo., p. 6.

The settlement officer would be unable then to follow Mr. Currie's procedure, *viz.*, "the rents *actually paid* by the cultivators of the different fields are what I have taken the basis of assessment; and it seems to me the only safe principle, for the ascertainment of the actual produce must be liable to very great uncertainties, and the productive powers of the different classifications of soil must vary much in the same class from contingencies of situation, facility of irrigation, &c., &c."

As to the results of the old system of trying to fix a rent for each field by elaborate calculations of produce, Mr. Colvin notes that "it was impossible to realize much more than three-fourths of the assessment."

As the Board of Revenue (N.-W. P.) declared in 1831, "to presume that the European officers of Government, who have no direct connection with agricultural operations, are qualified to assess the rent of every field in a village by classifications of soil and nice calculations of average produce and prices, even though the extent of stock and personal means of each ryot, which should have some influence at least in such matters, were known, is in our opinion, to presume that in support of which neither the actual results of experiment nor the fair deductions of reason can be adduced."

Even supposing however that trained assessors should be able to accurately determine what rise in rents would be justifiable at the expiry of a settlement, it is obvious that, while the enhancement of the revenue on the basis of compulsorily raised rents would relieve the landowner from suffering under a sudden diminution of his income, it would only transfer that portion of the burden, and the suffering from the landowning classes to the cultivators, from the idle to the industrious, from the working bees to the drones.*

The tenant's standard of comfort would be ruthlessly lowered, and his income would now be suddenly reduced; for thirty years he would have lived in comfort virtually as a landowner; he would now be abruptly dashed down to

* It may be thought that the interests of the landowners are deemed of far more importance than those of the tenants; on the contrary, attention has been drawn to the intimate connection between a rack-revenue and a rack-rent. At present the Government allows the settlement officer to rack-revenue the landowner, but, when he in his turn tries to transfer the burden to the tenantry, the Government in alarm calls on the Collector, not the settlement officer, for an explanation. The question how the tenantry can best be protected against rack-renting may soon become a pressing one. Instead, however, of converting them into temporary landowners, it would seem advisable that the rent courts should be invested, first, with discretionary powers in the matter of ejectment and as a necessary consequence; second, with similar powers in the matter of permitting enhancement of rent against the wishes of the cultivator, but these questions are too important to be more than hinted at in a note. At present it is indispensable to rein in the settlement officer, for he is, it is to be feared, the great rack-renter.

the level of a cottier. He would be rack-rented directly by Government officials, instead of as now as indirectly through the landowners, and we should render our rule directly hateful to the industrious tillers of the soil, while we should probably fail to really benefit the landowners.

Supposing that the assessor has been able to devise correct rent-rates for the thirteen classes of soil alluded to on a former page, *viz.* :—

Gowhan, 1*st.*	Terai, 2*nd.*
Gowhan, 2*nd.*	Dry domati, 1*st.*
Gowhan, unirrigated.	Dry domati, 2*nd.*
Irrigated domati, 1*st.*	Dry bhoor, 1*st.*
Irrigated domati, 2*nd.*	Dry bhoor, 2*nd.*
Irrigated bhoor.	Dry bhoor, 3*rd.*
Terai, 1*st.*	

and supposing, that all the land has been accurately mapped out into these different classes, what would the settlement officer do, if the cultivators refused point-blank to take his generous leases ? Why should they accept them ? It seems, for instance, incredible, that they would meekly agree to pay 88 per cent. more than they are now giving ; they might obstinately object that the assessor was dealing not with figures but with men, and that they could not afford to pay the revised rates. Would the State dare to aid the landlord to openly drive his tenants into the degraded condition of miserable, poverty-stricken, rack-rented cottiers? The Government may be strong enough to collect the existing rents of each pargana through the village accountants and Kanungos, if the landowners refuse to accept the offered revenue-engagements ; but what could it do, if the tenants organized a strike ? It can legally turn out the landowners, if they refuse to accept the leases ; but if it oust the cultivators, what class is it to substitute for them ?*

* The Chief Commissioner, on p. 17 of Oudh Revenue Report for 1872, notices that in Kheri "there has been practically a revolt against the late settlement officer's assessments," and the Government was obliged to direct a revision. Suppose the tenants followed suit ; they do practically by refusing to pay the enhanced rents.

The State would, it would seem, have either to remain content for the future with a very small increase of the revenue, or, if it persisted in its direct attempts to forcibly rack-rent the tenants, it would inevitably meet with strong opposition, and its schemes would receive the universal condemnation of all classes in England and India.

It is clear that if the State raises the land-tax on the basis of rents fixed by its own officers, it must in justice aid the landowner to collect them. If the tenants refuse or neglect to pay, the revenue demand must each year be proportionately reduced; Government officers must be ordered

---

It must not be supposed that tenants are so willing to accept leases in all districts as is here supposed even for these existing rents; they dislike to be bound down by a written agreement, in regard to which they are always very suspicious; it would be a work of considerable delicacy to induce the tenants-at-will as a body to accept written engagements even to pay low rents for a fixed term of years.

In some districts in Oudh, a register called the "tasfya lagan" or settlement of rent was drawn up at the end of settlement. In these quasi-rent-rolls the subordinate officials (Sadr Munsarim and Munsarim) with the patwari were supposed to make out a complete revised rent-roll for each village in the presence of and with the consent of the tenantry, but it was found that this so-called settlement of rents in most cases settled nothing; the cultivators either refused to attend at all, or, if they came, they refused to agree to any enhancement of rent; even if they did agree to pay, they as a fact paid no more than the landowner had collected previous to reassessment. The settlement officer had no compulsory powers even to fix rents, and even supposing he had been authorized by law to arbitrarily fix such a rent, although the cultivators refused to agree to his decisions, how could he gurantee the realization? The State could scarcely force a tenant to pay a rent to which he never assented, by selling at auction that tenant's personal chattels by attaching that tenant's crops, or by confining that tenant in the civil jail; in every legal code the consent of both parties is required to render a contract valid.

The landowner holds his estate subject to the due payment of the land-tax fixed by the Government; if he refuses to contract to pay the fixed sum, he is entitled to an allowance of $\frac{1}{10}$th of the rental, but the cultivator leases his fields on no such terms; his rent is a mere question of contract.

to harry and worry the cultivator, incessant inquiries in regard to rent-collections will be inevitable and the State must assume the rôle of a harsh, relentless, grinding landowner, while the landowner will be degraded to the position of an unproductive pensioner on Government bounty.

There are many other serious objections to this scheme, as, for instance, that it will create a large class of under-tenants claiming various rights and privileges unrecognizable by rent courts, while it will inevitably change the tenants themselves into temporary landowners, who, on the strength of their guaranteed tenure for thirty years, will mortgage and sell their lease-rights and their seer fields to strangers, to kinsmen, to money-lenders, and to sub-tenants, but it is unnecessary to refer to these obvious objections further.*

It does not seem possible, therefore, to attempt more than to secure at the time of assessment a fixation of the rents

---

* The best proof of the difficulty of effecting an assessment of the kind proposed by Mr. Colvin is afforded by the apparent breakdown of the Bombay reassessments. According to the *Pioneer* which seems to be in the possession of authentic information, "it is no secret that during the last few years the Bombay revenue survey system has been on its trial. To fix the date of this probationary period more distinctly, we may point to 1868 when Sir Seymour Fitzgerald finally sanctioned the reassessment of the Judupoor Taluka, the first in that series of new thirty years' settlements of which was the renewal of the modern Bombay land-revenue organization. Since that date, there have been more or less in all the resettled Bombay Collectorates sundry unmistakeable premonitions, that the enhancements of the survey will ill-stand the rough and real test of actual levy and collection." This article of July 2nd, adds, that, early in last year, it had become plain to Sir Philip Wodehouse and his Council that these new assessments could not be collected (in the Hawli Taluka). "Close and searching investigation was made, and the results of his recommendation (Revenue Commissioner) were embodied in the remarkable Resolution of last October. In this, a general reduction of the new assessments in the three districts was ordered, and a rule laid down for future guidance, prescribing a certain percentage of enhancement as a maximum not to be exceeded in future reassessments." It seems that the original assessment was a rise of 98 per cent. and this was reduced to 75 per cent.

of the privileged tenantry, by whom of course are signified all those, whether ex-proprietors or merely cultivators, who have been decreed seer or rights of occupancy;* if the settlement officer succeeds in thus adjusting the rent demand payable by those tenants, whether under proprietary or otherwise, on the basis of the rents actually paid at the time of assessment by the tenants-at-will, he will have carried out a most important work, and it would seem that the Legislative Council acted wisely in thus limiting the powers of the assessor.

Sir William Muir, in his speech before the Legislative Council, pointed out† the objections to a thirty years' rent

---

by the Government; the new reductions do not appear to have been reported, as it is supposed that there is some hitch or a difference of opinion between the Bombay Government and the Government of India.

Where revenue or rent assessments are based entirely upon conjectural estimates of the increased value of landed property, their equitable character cannot be proved to demonstration. There will always remain a doubt whether they are justifiable.

* There is really no necessity for fixing the rents of occupancy tenants in this way; if they are below or above the allowed favorable rate, either the landowner or the tenant can sue for their enhancement, and it seems better to leave all questions of amendment of rent in the first instance to the parties themselves; if the rent-rolls are but fairly accurate, the rent courts can determine without difficulty any cases, which may come before them.

† Even this will be no child's play, as the editors of the N.-W. P. Revenue Act point out:—"It is indispensable that the classification of soils should be most accurate, and then that the devised rent-rates should be correct representations of the real rental; when these two preliminaries have been settled, a day is fixed, and the parties are summoned. The landholder will either refuse to be a party to the business, or he will demand preposterously high rates. The tenants, on the other hand, will offer rates as absurdly low. The settlement officer will then come forward as arbitrator with the leases drawn up at the proposed rates, and after much bickering and bargaining, and explanations given to both parties, the matter can be generally arranged *in a few days*. But all depends on the fairness of the rates proposed, and the correct classification of the soils,"—Note to Section 74, Messrs. Crosthwaite's edition, Calcutta, 1875.

assessment even for the privileged tenants, and the Act consequently limits the period of fixation to ten years. He is reported to have said that "it would have been open to the British Government on its first accession to have laid down the principle, that rent and revenue were to be fixed for counterminous periods, nay, at a much later period, while the relative rights of landlord and tenant were as yet hardly settled by the administration of a fixed and uniform system, this might have been possible. Forty years ago the proposal was urged by Mr. Robert Mertins Bird, and was then fully discussed by the Government of India and its chief officers; and the conclusion was then deliberately come to, that such a course was inconsistent with the rights of the zemindars, and the prevailing condition of the cultivator; on the decision that rent was open to enhancement rested the whole revenue system of these provinces. To have now declared that rent and revenue to be equally fixed for the same term would not only have uprooted the revenue system of half a century, and created new and unexpected rights, but it would have injured and abated the landed title, which had grown up under that system. Properties had passed from hand to hand, estates had been sold both for Government balances and for decrees of court, rights and expectations had grown up and become matured under the system of a modified power of enhancement to the level of prevailing rates of rent. For a great and imperious political object, indeed, it might have been open to the Government even at the expense of these expectations to have altered the system. No legislative enactment had expressly defined the rights of the zamindars in this respect, or limited the power of Government to interfere for the protection of the ryot. But he (Sir. W. Muir) submitted that no such emergency existed, and that it would have been in the last degree inexpedient and unwise to have reversed the policy on which the relations of landlord and tenant had now for so long a time adjusted themselves."

These objections cannot, it is true, be deemed in any way conclusive, if it becomes necessary to legislate in the protection of tenants-at-will, in order to defend them from excessive rack-renting, since it has always been at least in theory a principle of our administration, that the landowners are to be restrained from extortion, still they are well worthy of mature consideration.

As a panacea for the evils incidental to our system of temporary assessments, it has been proposed to introduce the simple remedy of permanent settlements. There is no doubt that a permanent settlement would remove most of the evils resulting from our present system; there would be no sudden change caused in the circumstances of the landowners by the immediate introduction of a heavily enhanced tax; there would be no flood of corrupt and greedy native officials deluging the country at fixed intervals; there would be none of that general unrest and discontent, which precede the arrival of the "Hakim Bundobust" and of his staff, and which continue to be felt without abatement throughout the prolonged stay of that learned assessor. If, moreover, the tax was at the outset fairly assessed, there could be no outcry that the Government was ruining the landed classes by the heavy pressure of its revenue demand or by the unyielding character of its system of collection. Experience would seem to show that here its benefits would cease, and that it would in no way tend to induce landowners to apply their energies and their capital more extensively than they do at present to effect improvements in their property.

The failure of the Bengal Permanent Settlement in this respect is well known. Sir W. Muir, in a minute recorded by him on the 15th December 1861, remarked that one of the benefits which would result from the permanent fixation of the land-tax was "prosperity arising from increased motives of improvement and expenditure of capital;" but in his minute of March 1874 he records that he has seen reason to question whether, in the present condition of the agricultural population, this benefit is sensibly felt. He goes on to note that "the evidence for Azimgarh tends to show that there is no material difference in the prosperity or improvement of estates permanently assessed, as compared with those side by side with them under temporary settlement. No doubt in the progress of the country the time may be looked for when more enlightened ideas will prevail, and the owners of land will devote capital to agricultural and economical improvements. But the Lieutenant-Governor is bound to say that as yet there is little sign of this. The argument therefore under this head must be held wanting in force at the present time."

It is futile however to debate the advantages and disadvantages of a permanent settlement, so long as the scheme is financially impossible;* the land-tax is the only permanent and reliable source of income in this country, and, until other sources of remunerative taxation can be discovered, it is idle to suppose that the State can afford to dispense with its portion of the certain future increase in the rentals of the landed estates of Upper India.

---

* This was Sir Donald Macleod's objection to a permanent settlement. "He considered that it would be a mistake to declare permanent the money assessment of any land whatever, because money is an unreliable standard of value. Fifty years hence, if the demand assessed upon land represents but half the real value it did, when first assessed, it will be a matter of the utmost difficulty to find other sources, from whence the enormous deficit can be supplied, and the effort to realize it will be attended with exceeding danger. But Sir Donald added, if, instead of using a cash standard, we were to employ some other standard, supplying a correct measure of the increase of value, such as labor, and the price of corn, he would be entirely in favor of permanency of settlement, wherever the cultivation had attained to the required proportions."—P. 18, Material and Moral Progress of India, 1872. It has been calculated that but for the permanent settlement the Indian revenues would defray all expenditure, even if the whole receipts of the opium-tax were abandoned.

Holding, therefore, that the question of the introduction of permanent settlements is one for future generations, it will be advisable now to seek some remedies for the admitted evils of the existing system of revenue assessment, and a cursory glance at the memorandum published by Mr. A. Colvin enables any one to detect the main cause of the present unsatisfactory results of our assessment system. Settlement officers plod over their soils, exercise their wits over irrigated and unirrigated rates, compile laborious and often quite untrustworthy mountains of statistics, deduce scores of so-called average rent rates for a dozen different classes of soils, impose an enormously increased tax, and unsettle a district for years, simply because that they feel unable to accept the rent-rolls filed by the landowner as conveying any correct idea of the real assets. It is impossible, after reading this memorandum, to avoid feeling an unpleasant misgiving, that our assessments, thus framed, are little less than dangerous leaps in the dark.

If the rent-rolls could be received as representing with fair accuracy the assets of an estate, it is obvious that the costly machinery at present employed could be altogether dispensed with. There need be no expensive surveys or measurements, no laborious inquiries extending over a decade, no fresh classification of soils, no statements of average rent-rates, and above all there need be no misgivings in respect to the adequacy or the inadequacy of the revised tax; a whole district could be reassessed in a year or two by a single officer aided by the proper assistants to such work, namely, the Pargana Kanungos.

So far as my own limited experience goes, I believe that as a rule the village rent-rolls fairly represent *the rents paid in cash by the tenants-at-will;* or could with a little vigilance be made to do so; of course the ground in the cultivation of the proprietors is entered as paying only a nominal sum, and no assets are returned for rent-free holdings, religious endowments; lands held by village servants as the watchman of the crops, fields granted to old retainers, and other temporary or permanent alienations of these kinds. Where the rents are paid in kind, the rent-roll is undoubtedly an untrustworthy guide, but it could readily, with a little supervision, be made a more correct register of grain receipts. At present the village accountant is, as often as not, absent when the produce is distributed, and no one takes any trouble to ascertain what the real outturn of the crop has been: when the season arrives for the filing of the rent-roll, a rough guess is made, and no further thought is given to the matter.

Grain-rented villages may be thus classified :—

I. Those casual villages in a circle or tract where the lands of most of the villages pay rent in cash, and this class may be further sub-divided :—

(*a.*) Villages where all the land except the sugarcane and market-garden cultivation is grain-rented.

(*b.*) Villages where only the outlying sandy or hard clay lands or fields exposed to the ravages of wild beasts, are grain-rented.

II. Those lying in a pargana, all the villages of which, without exception, are grain-rented; as for instance the Tarai of Gonda and Bharaich.

Now for the first class it is quite sufficient, if the village accountant gives in an accurate return of the lands under cultivation. The assessing officer is able to judge with fair correctness, what rates such lands could bear, by comparing them with the cash-rented lands of a neighbouring village. The only point is to bear constantly in mind the necessity of being light for these inferior grain-paying fields. Similarly, the Collector knows, that the grain-rented village cannot deserve much consideration, if the owners of the cash-rented villages around it have collected their rents and paid up their revenue in full. But for grain-rented parganas or other tracts, the village accountant should be directed to show in his rent-roll the crop grown on each field, and to file an estimate of the total outturn for each cultivator's holding, while the Kanungo should, after a little time, be able to note pretty correctly, what, in his opinion, had been the average outturn for each crop in the different classes of soil. A register of the prices current in the different market towns of the sub-division could be maintained at the Tahsil.

It is admitted that assessments should be based on the actual rentals of landed estates, but little attempt has hitherto been made to secure annually the correct compilation of the village rent-roll; the accuracy of this return depends solely on the character of the village accountant, and, as soon as filed in the district office, it is consigned to the records and to oblivion. It is obvious that if only the cash rents paid by ordinary cultivators could be correctly obtained, the rest of the cultivated area could be assessed without the slightest difficulty by a mere process of analysis, comparison, deduction and addition.*

* It may be said that the settlements of those districts in Oudh, where the assessments were framed with the best attention to the rents entered in the village rent-roll, have almost alone stood the test of the last four years; I refer to the settlements of Rai Bareli and Partabgarh, Sultanpur and Unao.

On turning over the pages of Mr. Colvin's memorandum, it seems, that the rent-rolls filed by the landowners of Etawah, for instance, were reasonably reliable, for the settlement officer records that (p. 40) "the information thus obtained, went, as I have before said, to confirm the accuracy of the patwari's papers;" on p. 54, the settlement officer of Bareli notices that he found "the entries of amount of land and rents of assamies in the village papers were exceedingly correct *as far as they went* (the italics are his own.) The fraud in these papers was chiefly of two classes :—

(*a.*) A portion of the cultivated area and the rents chargeable on it were excluded from the jama-bandi and entered as fallow.

(*b.*) A large amount of land held by cultivators at the village rates was entered as seer at nominal rates.

In both cases the proportions of asamiwar collections to the extent of assamie's cultivation, as entered in the papers, remains unaltered;

It is immaterial however to dispute whether the rent-rolls as yet are fairly correct or not; for it is proposed, that

---

and by dividing the one by the other, the general rate of rent in the village is ascertained. The application of this rate to the cultivated area, as found by survey, will give a close approximation to the real village rental."

So in Furruckabad it is recorded (p. 36):—"This agreement and disagreement was to my mind a satisfactory proof of the tolerably accurate character of the declared rent-roll. If false rent-rolls had been filed, the zamindars and patwaris would have coached up the cultivators to respond accordingly, and there would have been little disagreement." The Muzaffarnagar settlement officer notes (his being apparently a grain-rent district) that the village papers showed the ratio of crops in different years, but they did not show them classified by soils; he considered (p. 23) that the patwaris registered accurately the kind of crop grown, but the record produced was quite untrustworthy. Similarly, the settlement officer of Saharunpur seems (p. 13) to have found the cash rents entered in the village rent-rolls formed a tolerably sure basis for calculation, after eliminating the rates paid by exceptionally favored cultivators, and it seems that even accepting the produce returns as given in these papers, the jama would only have been one-half lakh below what he considered the proper amount, and the difference was doubtless attributable to the fact, that the recorded seer produce was of course purely nominal.

The settlement officer of Mainpuri describes his excellent system on p. 37, *viz.*:—"The first thing I set about was to discover on what jama-bandis reliance could be placed as far at least as the rents paid by *bonâ fide* cultivators were concerned. I had already a fair idea of those villages, where the relations between the zamindar and assamies were not of such a friendly nature as to admit of entries of rent other than those actually paid. This did not prevent me from making further investigations. Act X has worked very well, in one respect at least, and zamindars are now very careful of recording rent at nominal rates, unless they are certain of their ryots; if they want to show a lower nikasi they adopt other means. They either throw land into seer, let it out on batai, or neglect entering in the patwari's papers former fallow as it was brought under cultivation. In a number of instances, the zamindars act as bankers to their assamies, and it was in those villages, that I found the jama-bandis most inaccurate." The settlement officer then goes on to say that he did not cease to make inquiries until he was satisfied that he had got correct returns, and, having at last obtained these, he derived his soil rates from them.

whether they are now accurate or inaccurate, a direct and sustained endeavour should be made by Government to secure every year a correct return of the rental, and of the agricultural condition of every village,* and that the future assessments should be based almost entirely on these annual rent-rolls; there is little doubt that this proposal could be carried into execution with very little expense, and that there would be no difficulty whatever in maintaining the scheme in efficient operation. The Oudh Govern-

---

The settlement officer of Unao records (p. 55, Unao Report), that as to the rents of tenants-at-will, we may be pretty sure, as a general rule, that the recorded rates are almost correct, and may be adopted with safety, "if capabilities and rates agree; if they disagreed, the settlement officer at once detected the flaw, and, if no satisfactory reason was discovered, he took the recorded rates of a neighbouring village."

I give an example of the proposed system in an Appendix. It is believed that Mr. Buck, C.S., of the North-West Provinces, has proposed a similar scheme, but I am unacquainted with the details of his proposal.

The system proposed is no new one; it was devised and worked in Unao with excellent results by Mr. Clifford, now Magistrate and Collector of the Moradabad district, and after his departure from Oudh, it was continued in Unao by his successor Mr. Maconochie.

* Since this was written, the North-West Provinces Board of Revenue has issued very elaborate rules for the correct annual compilation of the village papers. Unfortunately the N.-W. P. Government, instead of making the Collector responsible, has created a new department for the supervision of this work.

So far back as 1822, Mr. Holt Mackenzie urged the necessity of establishing "the patwari office on a proper footing" and of allowing these officials "under the character of joint servants of the people, and the State a liberal income from the contributions of the cultivators and the grant of the Government," and then he considered that we should soon lay the foundation of a greatly improved system of administration, under which we should really know the people and their concerns, and be able truly to govern and protect them. Under such a system, the malguzars would no longer be enabled to usurp the property of the under-tenants, or force the village accountants to be the instrument of exaction and fraud."

ment has recently passed certain rules ordering that the rent-roll shall be filed at the Tahsil on a fixed date, and that it shall then be tested on the spot by the Pargana Kanungo; this is a step in the right direction, but much remains to be done before the correctness of the rent-roll can be considered above suspicion.

In the first place the Kanungo has no sufficient leisure for a really careful verification of the pargana rent-rolls; he has multifarious duties to perform at the Tahsil, he has become a mere hack-clerk, as often as not he is unable to read the character, in which the village accountant writes up his rent-roll, and his supervision must necessarily be of a hasty and perfunctory nature.

It is hopeless to expect that the Tahsil Kanungo can find time to thoroughly test the rent-rolls. It is suggested, therefore, that a special Kanungo, who should be a member of the hereditary pargana family, and who should be well acquainted with Kayathi (the character, in which the rent-roll is written), should be appointed either for each Tahsil,* or for each two or three parganas in proportion to their size, and having regard to the tenure of landed property, that it should be this officer's sole duty to secure the correct compilation of these annual returns; that all the village accountants should be placed under his control; that every rent-roll should be personally tested on the spot; and that, in addition to the rent-roll, it should be his duty to see that the other annual statements, connected with the rent-roll, are correctly prepared and duly submitted. One of the

---

* The Government profits from the dastak fund would in Oudh nearly defray the cost of the required establishment. In 1871-72 the surplus amounted to Rs. 9,541-5 and in 1872-73 to Rs. 6,642-2-5. It is calculated that the required staff would cost about Rs. 7,500 per annum.

In the N.-W. P. the profits from the fees levied for the issue of these writs of demand amounted on 1874 to Rs. 15, 706. It appears that the Board of Revenue thought at one time of reducing the fee charged from 12 As. to 8 As. (para. 152, Report Board of Revenue.)

District Assistant Commissioners or Extra Assistant Commissioners could be appointed to generally test the Kanungo's work during the cold weather tour.* Finally, the rent-roll should be signed by the village headman and by the village accountant, and the rent courts should be careful, that the former does not obtain a decree for any rent in excess of the sums entered in the rent-roll. Every village accountant should live in the village to which he is appointed. He should be regarded as the joint servant of Government and of the landowner: his pay should be secured by special orders, and half of the paid salary should be defrayed by the Government;† his work should be rewarded from time to time by small presents, and his signatures should be attached to all plaints for arrears of rent. His presence

---

* Of course it is not meant, that the Assistant Commissioner or Extra Assistant Commissioner should do more than see generally, that the Kanungo has actually made inquiries in the different villages, and has done his best to secure accurate returns. Little good can be done by the Assistant Commissioner or Extra Assistant Commissioner himself personally probing the cultivators; the best way would be to attach the Kanungo to the Assistant Commissioner's camp during the cold weather tour, so that the Assistant Commissioner might see the former at work.

A writer to the *Pioneer* (September 2nd) suggests that a competent officer should be appointed to each district to survey and record all changes, fiscal and geographical, and he thinks that such professional surveyors could be secured on Rs. 400 or 500 per mensem. It would, probably, be sufficient to appoint one such officer for every four districts and to have the khusrahs or other survey papers amended once in every ten years, except in exceptionally jungle districts, where much land is yearly broken up.

† As for instance his pay could be treated as part of the annual revenue demand and it could be collected with the kists, as is done, it is believed, in the North-West Provinces, but not in Oudh or the Punjab.

In the North-West Provinces, however, the landowner is saddled with the whole cost of the accountant's pay, which frequently means the levy of a tax up to 6 per cent. on the land revenue; it is therefore a most oppressive item in a landowner's expenses.

should also be required at all the grain distributions, and all the crop valuations (kankuts).*

The other papers which should be submitted with the rent-roll are most important; they are technically known as the wasilbaki assamiwar, or the schedule of rent collections, and rent arrears for the preceding year; the milan khusrah, or the statement showing the amount of land under cultivation, the extent of new fallow, and of culturable waste, in short, complete details of the agricultural condition of the village, and thirdly the khewat or register of co-sharers. As will be shown the documents are especially necessary if the Collector is to personally superintend the collections of revenue, if he is to be anything more than a mere tax-gatherer, if in short it has been considered proved that the rigidity and the unyielding severity of our system of revenue collection is an evil, which deserves and admits of a remedy.

It would be absurd, of course, to propose that future assessments should be based on the rent-roll, unless their preparation is carefully watched by Government officials. There seems no reason, why, under the system suggested, the village rent-rolls should not be rendered as accurate data for the revision of the land-tax, as the imperfect inquiries, and the inaccurate deductions of the settlement officers; in the former case the assessments would be unmistakeably based on actual facts, while in the second case it is liable to vary with the varying crotchets of each separate officer.†

---

* Kankut "is thus described in Notes on North-West Provinces, pp. 92-3, *viz.*:—"One degree distant from the payment of rent on kind is the custom of taking the money value of an estimated share of the crop. When the crop is nearly ready to be cut, the landlord or his agent accompanied by the cultivator and some of the most respectable tenants, goes to the field and estimates the yield. The landlord's share is thus commuted to a money payment of its value at the market price."

† The settlement officer of Unao justly wrote that he could "conceive no system of arbitrary rates, by which I mean rates not actually

For the future assessments should be framed entirely on the village rent-rolls, unless the revising officer can show that such are not reliable, and in all cases the onus of proving, that they are untrustworthy, should be thrown upon his shoulders. If wilful attempts to deceive the assessor are detected, the landholders should be punished by the farm or temporary transfer of their estates.*

In proposing an assessment based on the existing rent-roll, one inevitable objection must be noticed. It will be urged that under this system it would frequently happen, that the landowners would not raise a single rent, when the time for the expiry of the settlement drew nigh, and that, directly the land-tax was fixed, they would at once enhance all the rents paid by the tenants-at-will to the possible full rate. The State, therefore, would in this way be defrauded of a large and legitimate increase of revenue. It must be recollected, however, that the landowners of Upper India are far too greedy of present advantages to largely forego any possible increase of income, in consideration of a future and uncertain gain; at most they might cease to enhance within a few years of the termination of the settlement, but it would not have been possible to raise the rents to any vast extent within the short space of some five years. Moreover, particular landowners would not care

---

deduced from recorded rents, no matter how carefully, or scientifically prepared, giving anything like so correct a picture of the village. Differing as every village will do more or less, it is hardly possible to get one rate which can be applied fairly to all the villages in a circle, though with apparently the same class of soil and amount of irrigation."—P. 55, Unao Report.

* This course was suggested by the Governor-General in 1832:—"His Lordship is by no means satisfied that the second object could not be attained without measurement by requiring the proprietor or proprietors to whom the benefit of a long lease might be offered, to furnish a detailed ruqba (area) of their estates, and their estimated produce subject to the condition, that the lease should be cancelled at any time on the detection of any gross misrepresentation as to the quality, or quantity of the lands engaged for."

to show low rentals, since their attempt to deceive could readily be checked by a simple inspection of the rent-rolls of neighbouring villages, and they would have to forego any increased rental for nearly half the period of settlement, before they could expect, that these measures would largely affect the determination of the new assessment. The objection presupposes also a general conspiracy on the part of all landowners, large and small, to deceive the Government in regard to the rent-paying capabilities of their estates, and it is not credible that such a league would easily be formed. Even if an association of this kind was formed, it would always be competent to the Local Government to suspend the ordinary principles of assessment, and to issue special instructions for the revision of the land-tax in that locality. It is only in a very exceptional district, like that of Bolundshahar, that such a case is likely to occur.

On the average the rise in rents during the period of settlement will in the future not be very large. Now that the landowners of a district like Meerut have been so unpleasantly, yet so involuntarily, compelled, to exercise more energetically their unlimited power of rack-renting tenants-at-will, it is not probable that, after the revision of assessments now being conducted, there will not be many landlords, who are ignorant of, or are unwilling to bring into play, their powers in this matter of rent-enhancement.

In regard to this question, and, also to give more time to the landowners to make the necessary arrangements for the payment of an enhanced land-tax, it is further suggested that the revision-operations should be commenced in such time as to guarantee the completion of the re-assessment by the expiry of the current settlement. The State would then not lose so much by a system of progressive enhancement as it now does, when the new tax is not declared till some years after the expiry of the former assessment.

It is urged also that, considering the altered circumstances of the landed classes under our system of assessment and collection, it is inequitable to lay the whole burden of the payment of the village police on their shoulders. These rural custodians of the public peace have now become purely public servants. Under the native government they were the retainers of the landowner, and in obedience to his orders they kept watch over the crops and property of the villagers; they had not to report deaths to the Government police station, nor to prepare statistics for the registering of all female babies. They have now become a distinct police-service under the immediate control of the district police officers. The landowners have, therefore, been obliged to take into their service other resident villagers to execute the work which formerly the village watchman had time and disposition to perform, yet the State compels them to pay the whole cost of the village watchman now transformed into a Government police officer with multifarious public duties.

It was suggested, some years ago, by the settlement officer of Unao, that at re-assessment certain fields should be marked out and fixed as the rent-free holding of the village policeman; the fields were to be exempted from assessment, and they were to be carefully registered in the Government records.*

* The settlement officer's remarks are given in full, *viz*:—"These Pasis were and are still for the most part employed as village police; and most efficient watchmen they prove, when induced to act, either by fear or good treatment. At present, however, neither inducement is presented to them. Our Government does not allow their being punished, as they were in the Nawabi, when found negligent, but neither I venture to think, has it taken adequate precautions to see, that they are paid sufficiently and regularly; their remuneration being left entirely to the landowners, they in reality receive little or nothing from the majority; if the wage is given in land a portion in the outer Har, away from the homestead, is given to the chaukidar, and if in money, it is paid so irregularly, that the unfortunate recipient seldom receives above half, and, if he complains, is usually dismissed by his employer on some trumped-up accusation. The consequence of this is, that as a body, they are discontented, and until regularly paid, will remain inefficient, and the great promoters of crime. It might be

It must be recollected that in the Nawabi, these village watchmen were paid chiefly by the gift of varying amounts of grain from each cultivator or by the grant of a few rent-free plots. Now we, for the most part, compel the landowners to pay the salary of this class of old village servants in hard cash, and, if the required sum is not paid in full, the Collector can realize it by putting in force any of the coercive processes, which he could employ for the recovery of arrears of revenue. The cost, therefore, of these watchmen is a very oppressive additional tax on the landed classes.

If in every village a small parcel of land yielding an annual rent equivalent to the ordinary salary of a village policeman (24 to 36 rupees per annum) was thus set apart, the loss to the State would be insignificant, and the gain would be very great; if it was considered that the landowners should pay half the wages, the land could be assessed to the revenue, and the proprietor could be required to pay half that assessment to Government.

Again, the village accountant has become in fact a public servant; it is to him that settlement officers must

---

said that they are no worse off than in the Nawabi. It is impossible to continue Nawabi customs under our rule; and I do not hesitate to assert, that there can be no successful suppression of crime so long as the village police are left as at present. I would suggest that settlement officers should mark off certain field as the chaukidari jagir, and as Government expects more service from them, than in former days, these fields should be exempt from assessment. The loss would be small, while the gain, in having rural police partially paid servants of Government, would be great."—P. 168, Unao Report.

As Sir John Kaye noted in his History of the Administration of the East India Company (p. 264), "the establishment of a paid village police was still more generally unpopular" and it appears that the Lieutenant-Governor Mr. Robertson "had always been opposed to this measure. He expressed a strong opinion to the effect, that such a functionary as a paid watchman could never be acceptable to the people, even if it entailed no additional charge upon them." Even in 1851 A.D., the Court of Directors could only be "disposed to hope, that with careful supervision it may be found satisfactory to the people."

look in order to obtain accurate data for the fixation of the land-tax, and it is from him alone that the Collector can secure a correct compilation of the village records, whereas under the native administration he was merely the private servant of the landowner. As the correct performance of his duties will so greatly lighten the work of both these officers, as in fact the whole future success of our revenue system depends on the intelligence, honesty, and industry, with which his rent-rolls, and other registers will be compiled, it is only equitable, that the State should contribute its share to pay the salaries of these public officers.

Just as in the Nawabi the village policeman was paid an uncertain wage, as by the grants of rent-free holdings, or by the gift of some grain, so the village accountant lived in his master's house, and was generally fed and clothed at his master's expense; at most he received a small salary in grain, or each cultivator paid a small sum in cash, or a small share of the crop-outturn before its distribution between himself and the landowner. A forced payment of 6 per cent. on the gross assets under our system proves a new source of woe to the unfortunate landed proprietors. At least half the cost should in future be borne by the State, but the best plan would be to mark off certain fields for the support of the village accountant; for these plots the landowners should be required to pay only half the full assessment, and the village accountant could either cultivate them himself, or let them to residents of the village.

In regard to the assessment of the orchards, gardens, and small cultivated holdings of the residents in the small Mahomedan townlets, it might reasonably have been expected, that the Government would not have suddenly confiscated their prescriptive exemption from any payment of revenue. Considering their long immunity from taxation, and their reduced circumstances, it savoured of extreme harshness to assess these plots to the land revenue, and the Government would have shown a wise liberality in formally declaring, that the lands included within the boundaries of these townlets should not be brought within the operation of the ordinary rules of the settlement department. The loss to the imperial exchequer from the exhibition of this scanty generosity would have been very trifling, and the residents could have been required to contribute a small sum towards a local rate for the payment of the town police, and the necessary conservancy establishment in proportion to the average value of each individual holding.

Leniency in these cases was distinctly enjoined in 1822, when the Governor-General recorded a minute to this effect that "independently of the object of maintaining the higher class of the native community, it is the desire of Government that much consideration should be shown for persons, who have long enjoyed rent-free lands, whether in our old or in our more recently acquired provinces. Though the tenures may be invalid and abusive, it is not wise or humane to urge the Government rights to a length entailing the distress and ruin of individuals."

In conclusion it is strongly urged, that the Indian Government should declare formally, that it will not increase the land-tax, as now assessed for the term of the present settlement, in the disguised shape of cesses. Sufficent evidence has, it is hoped, been adduced to show that the landholders of Upper India are already taxed to the utmost limit of their capacities, and that, under whatever name it may please Indian statesmen to christen their extra taxation, whether as cesses, local rates, educational fees, subsidies, compulsory canal-fees or road funds, any additional impost will prove a burden, which in the face of the demands already made from the owners of landed property, we cannot equitably impose upon their estates.*

* The question is not, whether we levy a cess on the landowners *quâ* zamindars or not; the point is that when we fixed the land-tax at 50 per cent. we did so, because it was considered, that the landed classes *could not* pay a large percentage; if we go on adding cess to cess, we practically

It is not just that they should bear these excessive burdens, yet in the report presented to Parliament to show the moral and material progress of India in 1871-72, it is recorded, that "by a recent despatch from the Secretary of State, a change has been made with regard to the settlement of the cesses, for, while the amount of the land revenue is fixed absolutely for the period of the settlement, the amount of cesses is declared to be open to revision from time to time, at the discretion of the Local Government."

What is this but an open return to the practices of the native rulers, who, under various pretences, exacted an additional cess from the landowners, whenever they were pressed by monetary difficulties ?*

Lord Northbrook has shown firmness and wisdom in setting his face steadily against all proposals for exacting a larger revenue from the land, than assessments calculated at half-assets will afford. When the present Viceroy lays down the reins of his high office, it will be his enlightened policy in regard to the collection and assessment of the land

---

return to the 65 per cent. rule, which was distinctly abandoned, because it took too large a share of the assets; if, as Sir J. Strachey holds, we tax the landholders with cesses *not* as landholders but as ordinary inhabitants, then the cess should be levied equally from all classes of the community. As matters now stand, the well-to-do tenants, the village shop-keepers, and money-lenders, and the village artisans escape scot-free, yet the cesses are expended in schools, roads, post offices, bridges, &c., which are intended for the good of the whole community, and not merely of the landed classes. While we declared that the land-tax should be reduced to 50 per cent. we added cesses, patwari's rates, village police rates, and local rates, so that the proportion of the assets payable to the State remains as before.

* "The Sovereign's full share is now reckoned at one-half. This increase has been made, not so much by openly raising the king's proportion of the crop as by means of various taxes and cesses, some falling directly on the land, and others more or less circuitously affecting the cultivator. Besides these, there are arbitrary cesses of both descriptions, which were professedly laid on for temporary purposes, but have been rendered permanent in practice."—Elphinstone's India, p. 76, Chapter II.

revenue quite as much as his administration of the famine operations in Bengal, or his financial policy, that will constitute his chief claim to consideration as a prudent and successful Indian statesman. When Sir George Campbell offered to the Legislative Council various suggestions for securing a larger revenue from the landed classes, the Governor-General expressed his own view in a concise speech :—" I wish to observe, that, in my opinion, there is no necessity for imposing new taxes in India, and revisions of the land settlement should be conducted with great moderation and consideration for existing interests."*

It is probably not too much to say, that, had Lord Northbrook been Viceroy in 1869, there would have been no such over-assessment, as has been described on the earlier pages of this volume, and it may be doubted, whether the Local Rates Acts would ever have passed into law.

* The firm support, which the Viceroy gave to the determination of the Oudh Government to secure an equitable *land-tax* for that province, and to remove difficulties which were fast ruining the landed-classess, has enabled that administration to effect many necessary changes even at a large sacrifice of revenue.

CHAPTER V.

PROPOSED CHANGES IN OUR SYSTEM OF COLLECTION OF THE LAND-TAX, AND IN OUR REVENUE ADMINISTRATION.

"So let the change which comes be free
To ingroove itself with that, which flies,
And work a joint of State, that plies
Its office, moved with sympathy."

In the third chapter of this volume an endeavour was made to show, that at any rate Government is to blame for the embarrassments of the landowners in so far as it neglects to make due provision for unusual calamities, in so far as the Collector's procedure is dilatory and incomplete, in so far as the officials injudiciously stretch the principle of joint responsibility, in fact, in so far in fact as the Collectors, and Tahsildars of land-revenue are, owing to the press of other work and the absence of reliable information, necessarily inefficient and perfunctory in the discharge of their duties.

The plea on the part of the Collectors is plain and direct; they answer, and with justice so far as they are officers belonging to the non-regulation provinces, that they are necessarily ignorant of the state of their districts, since, owing to the exigencies of the public service, they are being constantly transferred from one station to another, and that, even if they were allowed to remain in any one district for a longer period than is now usual, they have in these provinces so many pressing duties of other kinds to perform as judicial officers, as controllers of the local funds, as the responsible guardians of the local treasury, as the superintendents of local works, as vice-presidents of the municipalities, and as the official heads of the police, that they have no leisure for such a minute supervision over the collection of the land-revenue as is here suggested.*

* In Oudh, the Central Provinces, and the Punjab, the Magistrate and Collector (who is one and the same officer as he is in the North-Western-

No one will deny, that these apologies are amply sufficient to vindicate these officers; in the Punjab the present Lieutenant-Governor has succeeded in relieving his Collectors by inducing the Government of India to sanction the organization of some extra judicial staff or increased judicial service; if the change is required in the Punjab, it is still more urgently needed in Oudh, a newly annexed province, where it is necessary to watch with attention the effect of our laws and of our system of administration, while in it also the districts are larger, and the population is denser than in the Punjab. The separation of judicial and executive functions is merely a question of time; the change is unfortunately only

---

Provinces) has, in addition to the duties which appertain to that office in the North-West Provinces, to sit as an appellate court for civil suits, and as a court of original civil jurisdiction; he has also a larger criminal jurisdiction in the less grave sessions cases. So the Commissioner conducts the duties not only of the North-West Provinces Commissioner proper, but of the North-West Provinces Sessions Judge.

The duties of the North-West Provinces Collector are thus given in Messrs. Crosthwaite's North-West Provinces Revenue Act, p. 9:—

He is Collector of the land revenue.

He is Registrar of the landed property in the district.

He is Judge between landlord and tenant.

He is the Ministerial Officer of the courts of justice.

He is Treasurer and Accountant of the district.

He is the Administrator of the district excise.

He is ex-officio President of the local rates committee.

He is referee for all questions of compensation for lands taken up for public purposes.

He is agent for the Government in all local suits to which it is a party.

He is referee in the designing and carrying out of local public works, and in practice he is manager of the estates of minors under the Court of Wards. Then in addition to these miscellaneous executive duties he is the Magistrate of the district, and as such he is the Chief Police Magistrate and a Crimiual Judge up to certain limits.

He is also the head of the Police and he is ex-officio President of all the municipalities.

feasible at the cost of an increased staff, or at least by the grant of adequate salaries for those, who may select the judicial branch of the service, and the Government of India may naturally hesitate to increase its establishments at the present juncture, when it has incurred an immense expenditure in order to feed the famine-stricken millions of Bengal. It might at any rate be possible, for a very small cost, to augment as in the Punjab the salaries of the senior assistants, and they could then be invested with appellate judicial powers: the Collectors could in this way be relieved of a considerable amount of judicial work.

There can be no question however that the Government is bound to use its best efforts to render the duties of the Collector lighter, if not by relieving him of part of the judicial work, at least by giving him all possible help so as to enable him to discharge his duties with greater promptitude and efficiency. It is indisputable that much mismanagement and harshness at the instance of native subordinates now disgraces our administration; if the village records were constantly prepared, as has been here proposed, such cases should never occur; if the Collector had in his office, in addition to the description of the village contained in statement* No. II, a correct rent-roll, and also returns to show the amount of cultivated and uncultivated land, the fields, which had fallen out of cultivation owing to floods, drought or cattle disease, the collections, the balances due from the cultivators and the number and circumstances of the proprietors, he could have no difficulty whatever in ascertaining at once whether, and if so in what manner the revenue arrears should be collected or whether the landowners could reasonably ask for some temporary, or permanent relief. In the event also of the wilful default of any one co-sharer the Collector could by an inspection

* This is a record, in which the settlement officer writes down the result of his inspection of each village, when he visits them prior to revising their revenue payments.

of the register of shares be able to judge, whether it would be possible to transfer the defaulter's share to any other member of the village community, whether there is any mortgagee, who could be induced to take the land for a term of years, or whether the balances could only be realized by a sale or farm of the property.* Further the Kanungo should be restored to his old position of revenue adviser to the Collector and his assistants; he has under our system of administration been degraded to the level of a hack-clerk at the Tahsil office; he has lost all knowledge of his sub-division and his former intimate acquaintance with the circumstances of the landed proprietors and the condition of the properties and tenantry is fast becoming a thing of the past. It has therefore been proposed, that a special Kannungo should be now appointed to aid the Collector in his executive duties as a revenue officer. It is the duty of the Government to do justice between man and man and between itself and the individual tax-payer in its administration and collection of the land revenue; it is contrary to public policy and to the best interests of the State that its officers should year by year compulsorily exact so large

* While an enormous and very expensive establishment has been entertained at each revision of settlement to prepare vast quantities of vernacular registers for record in the Zillah office, not a single register written in English has been prepared for the future information of the Collector. The settlement officer hands over to the latter a largely enhanced land-tax to collect, but he gives to him small aid towards the easy discharge of this work; every district officer should have been supplied with an alphabetical English register mahalwar (*i.e.*, per estate) showing for each mahal, its position, the names of the proprietors, the thoks and pattis (divisions and sub-divisions), the headmen, the constitution of the estate (whether lands are divided or held in common), the character of the proprietors, and tenantry, and a short summary of the revenue history. This should be maintained by each Collector up to date, and with such a register in his possession the Collector would have small difficulty in dealing with cases of revenue arrears; he would not have to break his heart over the interminable and unintelligible "kaifyats" (reports) from the Tahsildars, and an immense saving of time would be effected.

a portion of the rentals of all landed property, and that they should at the same time refuse to be more than mere tax-gatherers, turning aside neither to the right hand, nor to the left hand, so long as they can screw the full tail from the tax-payer. The State is co-sharer with the landowner, and it is bound to take a due interest in and to exercise a strict watch over the latter's management of the common property of both; under no other theory can our rule be aught else than lamentably odious to the landed classes, for under our existing system there can be no doubt, that great injustice is done year by year, and that harshness, and even cruelty is frequently displayed in our present method of collection.

Allusion has already been made to the greater suitableness, and therefore also to the greater popularity of the native method of assessment and collection, in so far as it guarded more carefully against waste and improvidence on the part of the landowners by a more prompt collection of the share of the rents, which were considered due to the State, in so far as it allowed no sudden changes in the circumstances of the revenue payers, and in so far as its system of administration more frequently entailed a temporary rather than a permanent dispossession of the landowner, as a punishment for his failure to pay up the balances of land revenue. The complete and permanent loss of a landed estate, though by no means unknown, was not nearly so common as it is under our rule, and it is proposed that we should return, as far as is possible, to the native system.

Direct management of encumbered property in land is only possible in cases, where the estate is a large one, or at least where it is an entire estate, and not a fractional share of a village; it is not desirable, that Government officers should attempt to interfere in the management of villages held by large proprietary bodies, nor could the State provide a sufficient staff of officers for this duty; it would be quite impossible for the Collector to properly superintend the management of a hundred different estates in different parts of his district, in one village a share of two annas, in another a plot of seer, in a third a dozen acres held with rights of occupancy, in a fourth a religious endowment, and in a fifth a few fields held on a birt title. Those who have ever acted as Collectors of Revenue, or as their assistants, know how difficult it is to manage even one or two little attached estates, how the ex-proprietors will not pay the full rent, how the expenses of management swallow up the profits, how the tenants league with the debtor and pay him surreptitiously part or all of their rents, and how the whole village sets itself against the intruding Government manager; it is possible of course to manage satisfactorily large estates, or even whole villages, but similar attempts to manage small shares, or plots of land would inevitably result in disastrous failure; there would be no means at hand for the intimidation of the dispossessed owner; even the Government revenue or the current rents due to the proprietor, were the estate an under proprietary one, would be with difficulty realized, and Government would be saddled with the management of all the insolvent estates throughout the country, for, if only the estate could pay its way, neighbours, farmers, cultivators or money-lenders would have been willing to take the lease for a term of years.

It is highly desirable that the system of temporary attachment should be attempted in all cases, in which it can reasonably be expected, that the debt will be realized with interest in a limited number of years, but any more general extension of this system would assuredly prove a curse instead of a blessing to the country; the sooner ruined landowners lose their estates, the better it is for Government and for every one else; it is impossible to do more than to provide that all sales of land in execution of decrees shall, as is the rule in Oudh and the Punjab, receive the sanction of the highest judicial authority; a rule of this kind affords quite a sufficient check against indiscriminate and unnecessary sales of hereditary estates, and it is always open to the controlling authority to allow the outgoing landowner to retain a right of occupancy in his seer.*

It is suggested, that the Government besides temporarily attaching landed estates, whenever this plan is feasible, should much more frequently than is at present the case, and *much more speedily* resort to the temporary transfer of shares to solvent co-sharers, to mortgagees, to the civil decree-holders, to a stranger, or in some few instances to a well-to-do cultivator. At present the revenue is collected by the Tahsildar in his own way and at his own time; his frowns and threats of sale by auction are usually sufficient at last to induce the landowner to clear off the arrears by begging a loan at usurious interest from the local money-lender. It is absolutely necessary for the Collector to act, before the landowner has become hopelessly involved, for then the liens on his land will render a temporary transfer impossible.

It is recommended that in a modified form a return should be made to the "malzamini" system of native government; the headmen of incorrigible defaulting villages could be called on to give security for tho punctual payment of the revenue; these sureties would usually be some well-to-do sharer, or respectable neighbour. On the default of the principal the arrears would be collected from the surety, and he, in consideration of his payment of the balance, would receive from the Collector possession of the estate for a fixed term of years. The advantage of this practice over the system of attaching a defaulting estate is obvious, and it is preferable to giving out the estate in farm, because first the surety would, prior to the default, take measures to induce the principal to be punctual in the discharge of the tax, and secondly because there would be no necessity for long reports and delayed references. Immediately the revenue fell due and the headman failed to pay it, the Collector would send for the surety, call upon him to pay

* The North-West Provinces Revenue Act grants for the future a right of occupancy, heritable and transferable, to all dispossesed landowners.

up the balance, and hand over the estate to him for a term of years to be fixed in proportion to the amount of the balance. Before farm can be sanctioned, it is necessary for the Collector to find a farmer, and then further delays take place before the sanction of the Local Government is obtained.

If the headman fail to obtain security, the Collector should be authorized to* temporarily transfer on farm the village or share, and, as there would be no arrears of revenue due to the State, there would be no difficulty probably in finding co-sharers or neighbours ready to take over the property for a term of years. During that period the dispossessed landowner should retain his seer at fixed favorable rates.

It may be doubted, whether the dates appointed for the payment of the revenue instalments are not fixed too late;†

---

* This would prevent practices of this kind, *viz.*:—"The dernier resort of sale cannot be worked, for the money-lender will advance to the amount of balance with the view of keeping the estate, which is his only security for the repayment of the debt due to him, in the possession of his debtor, and this will go on till the debtor is hopelessly involved."—P. 15, Revenue Report of Board of Revenue, N.-W. P., for 1874. Again:—"The remaining balance of Rs, 330 is on account of the now well-known village Ratnapur Sarayoor, in which the proprietor refuses to pay up the arrear, until forced by an order for sale, which he averts by paying up the arrears the day before the sale."—P. 24.

† It appears from the Oudh Revenue Report (1873) that it has been resolved to collect the revenue in eight instalments instead of four as an experiment in the Gonda district; the dates fixed are:—

Kharef (autumn) 8 annas.	15th October 2 annas 15th November 2 annas	15th December 2 annas. 15th January 2 annas.
Rabi (spring) 8 annas.	15th March 2 annas 15th April 2 annas	15th May 2 annas. 15th June 2 annas.

This is a step in the right direction, and the change will assuredly prove beneficial to the landowners and useful to the Collector.

At present the Collector must wait with his hands folded till the 15th November and the 1st May before he can call on a single landowner to pay a farthing, yet, as the rents begin to fall in about the middle of September and beginning of March, they are wasted by the landowners.

the landowners have too much time between the realization of their rents, and the necessary despatch of the revenue to the local treasury; the money meanwhile burns in their pockets, or else the money-lender is putting on the screw; and part of it at any rate is applied to other purposes, than to the prompt payment of the land-tax. The Tahsildar drivels on with his notices to pay (dastak) for two months or more after the kists have fallen due; the landowners finding, that their failure to obey the writs of demand is not attended with any worse consequences than the despatch of a fresh notice neglect to pay off the arrears, and it is not, till all their ready money has been spent, that the Collector wakes up, or the Tahsildar becomes frightened, and orders are issued for the arrest of the defaulter; then the latter to escape persecution has to borrow and mortgage to clear off the arrears.

The Tahsildar should not be allowed to issue more than two or three writs of demand; if they fail, the landowners should be sent without delay to the Collector, or at least a full report should be at once despatched to that officer for his orders; prompt action on the part of the Tahsildar and of the Collector is indispensable. Under our system landed property is changing hands with alarming rapidity, yet we flatter ourselves, that, because the Government has sold no estate for arrears of revenue, our assessments and our method of collection cannot be pressing heavily on the landed classes.

The Government dislikes to openly sanction compulsory transfers of property; it loves to show a fair statement con-

It may of course be objected, that there is no necessity for so many kists; this is a reasonable objection and, from the last Oudh Revenue Report just published, it would seem that the Chief Commissioner considered five would be sufficient, *viz.* two on the autumn harvest, two on the spring harvest, and one on the sugarcane.

It is not advisable to have too many kists, as every addition to their number multiplies registers and accounts, and indefinitely increases the routine work of the Collector and Tahsildar, besides necessarily augmenting the number of coercive processes.

taining no notice of coercive processes; it delights naturally to plume itself on the absence of any harshness on the part of its revenue subordinates; this mask must now be thrown aside; no hesitation should be shown in sanctioning proposals for transfers or farms, long and wearisome reports should be curtailed; when the Government has educated itself sufficiently to understand, that *coercive processes promptly carried out are the proper mode of dealing with cases of revenue arrears*, a real reform in our revenue system will have been brought into operation; *when we see statements full of reported farms and transfers, then we shall know, that the landed classes are being —not ruined—but preserved.**

Let us have no more nonsense. Let us face facts candidly: let us give relief at once, when relief is deserved, but let us also punish promptly, when punishment is required; in dealing out punishment, let us however recollect, that we have introduced into a newly conquered country an alien system of unswerving obedience to rules and regulations, and let us, where it is practicable, save the people from the results of their own mismanagement or extravagance. If it is possible, let us preserve an estate and save the property for the landowner's innocent descendants. In many cases it will be easy enough to find persons who will take over the estate, and who will consent to pay off the arrears either at once, or within a limited time; land-

* Sir John Strachey apparently disbelieves in the virtue of coercive processes, as he records that he wishes "to draw their particular attention (Board of Revenue) to the increased facility, with which coercive processes seem at present to be sanctioned, and to state that he looks with much disfavor on the growth of such a procedure; which in most cases, indicates careless and slovenly action on the Collector's part."—Para. 23, Review of Revenue Report, 1874. The Lieutenant-Governor's remarks may however have been penned with special reference to the writs of demand, rather than to the 47 transfers recorded.

It should be recollected, that under the native government nothing was more common than to hold an estate direct, to farm or transfer it for a term of years.

holders, who have shown themselves incompetent, should be reduced for a time to the position of cultivators on privileged rents, and it may reasonably be hoped, that their sons, taught by a sad experience, will learn to some extent the value of habits of ordinary prudence; land should not be sold, until other measures have proved impracticable, unless it is judged expedient to punish an exceptionably gross case of wilful default by a public sale of an estate; in such cases determined and immediate action is recommended as a warning to others; it is only a mawkish sentiment, which would maintain a ruined, or an obstinate revenue-payer in the possession of his ancestral estate.

The necessity for despatch in questions of this kind is self-evident; Collectors, or at least Commissioners should be allowed to sanction sales, transfers, and farms, or else long-winded reports should be eschewed and by a well-understood rule, revenue applications should be labelled "urgent," and they should be disposed of without delay by the officers, whose sanction is now required. Under the present rule the Collector's authority is so limited, that he has only power to suspend the collection of the tax to some later date within the revenue year (ending September 30th) or to temporarily attach a defaulting landowner's estate. He cannot transfer a share, farm a share, remit arrears, or permanently take under his charge any estate or portion of an estate without the sanction of the Commissioner and the Board of Revenue (or in Oudh the Chief Commissioner). As therefore none of these coercive processes can be put in force, until the Collector has forwarded to his superiors a long report, and until the sanction of these officers has been received, it is no matter for wonder, that Collectors prefer to make every effort to realize the tax by merely compelling defaulters to mortgage or sell, since they have no leisure for the compilation of the required report. It is not easy to understand, why Collectors should not at least be allowed to farm or transfer a share of an estate or a whole property, his orders being subject to appeal to the Commissioner

Before any thorough reform of the revenue system can be effected, the Collector's hand must be strengthened by the grant of authoritative jurisdiction on these matters; if he is competent to have charge of a district at all, he can be trusted to take, as a rule, proper measures in cases of default by the landowners; if he is incompetent, he should not obtain the appointment at all.

The system which forces landowners to pay up in each year a fixed sum, whether the season is blessed with abundant harvests or cursed with a complete failure of the crops has already been shown to be unsuïted to the natives of this country; the principle, that in the long run the number of good and bad years is about equal and that the extra gains in one year should be held to counterbalance the special losses in another may be theoretically correct, but it is forgotten, that our assessment, even where it is reasonable in amount, is not based on average receipts, but on nominal assets; instead also of allowing the payment of the total demand to be made at any time within three years or so, taking care of course to prevent the undue accumulation of balances, we compel the landowner to pay the same sum (and that sum an income tax) whether he is rich, or whether he is poor; our system of taxation is thereby rendered most oppressive; it takes large sums from the landowner at times, when he is most unable to pay them, and it leaves him in the possession of receipts, when he could easily be compelled to contribute a larger contribution to the State; for the natives of this country a land tax thus collected is in many years a tax not on income, but on capital, and this means, that the landowner is compelled to clear off his balances by raising loans at usurious interest. It should surely be our policy to require the landowners, so far as is possible, to pay the tax at the most convenient time, and this could easily be carried out in practice by a more frequent resort to suspensions in years of agricultural distress.

Even when the suspension of some arrears is allowed, the time within which the defaulter is directed to clear off the debt, is generally far too short; a respite of three months till the next harvest is of little use. It is absurd to suppose that the landowner will be able to liquidate the current demand, as well as the suspended arrears from one harvest; if relief is granted in this shape, the period of respite should be considerably extended; in short a more yielding system is required, if we continue to assess on nominal and not on average incomes.

In order to prevent the possibility of the loss to the State, it is further suggested, that a moderate yearly interest, say 5 per cent., should be levied on all suspended balances, until they are liquidated, and that this interest should be collected with the current revenue demand.

It will be objected, that, if we unbend in this way, we shall never induce the landowners to pay up the land-tax at all, that they will become quite demoralized, and that, relying on this unwonted generosity, they will always be in arrears; it is replied, that one of the proposed changes in our system is a prompt and determined punishment of all wilful defaulters, and that, so long as the village papers are kept up to date, the Collector can have no difficulty whatever in knowing, whether any particular landowner does, or does not deserve relief; if the Collector does his duty properly, and if he is firmly supported by Government, the landowner will soon realize the hopelessness of any attempts at deception. Those only would receive relief, who really deserved it, and all others would be promptly punished for their default by the permanent or temporary loss of their estate; the sale on the spot of a wilful defaulter's property would soon check recusancy.

At present the power of coercion allowed by law is as seldom directly used as in the corresponding relief jurisdiction of the revenue officers; if we extend relief to the deserving, we must at the same time exercise more rigour towards the refractory; under the existing system we chop and change; at one period rigorous collection is enjoined and at another mercy is all the cry; in one year the guilty and the innocent are equally punished, and in another year both are equally favored.

It would be well, if Collectors employed their assistants more systematically in revenue matters; each assistant should have the charge of a Tahsil; he should spend the whole cold weather in travelling through it, and it should be his business to make himself acquainted with the condition of the landowners and of the cultivators. Nothing can be more valuable than the cold weather tour, if the officer's time is properly employed; no one desires to see junior officers careering wildly through the villages on broken down ponies, alarming and unsettling their sub-divisions by conducting formal enquiries; the work of making acquaintance with the people is best done quietly with a gun or fishing-rod in one's hand; the assistant on returning to the station should be required to submit an account of his proceedings, and in a short time there would be in the Collector's office a complete and exhaustive description of the existing condition of his district; the Collector would no longer be compelled to act blindly on the report of his Tahsildar;* constant orders are issued for the employment of young officers in revenue cases, but, as many of them are required at the district office to sign money orders and to count stamps, the directions are disregarded.

Until the staff of the Collector is increased, and until he has at his command such a knowledge of the estates and landowners of his district, that he can at once decide on the proper course to pursue in the case of revenue arrears, the revenue administration will never be placed on a satisfactory basis. We can no longer continue to attempt to govern Indian districts with the old staff of subordinates under the changed circumstances of our rule, and in the face of

* The settlement reports soon become useless, and at best they fail to tell much of the existing condition of the landowners; they rarely see the light till many years after their compilation, and they only refer to the district, as it existed before the pressure of the revised assessment has begun to make itself felt.

the heavy routine work of the Collector's office. Until every landowner is assured, that he and his village are both well known at head-quarters, and that he has no hope of consideration unless he is really entitled to relief, until also he realizes, that voluntary defalcation means instant sale or farm, we shall never have an efficient and yet merciful collection of the land tax.

Having in this way endeavoured to render the Collector's work easier, an attempt should be made to smooth away some of the difficulties which beset the small landowners, the village communities of Upper India. I would specially urge the necessity for some simple Act which would give the Collectors power to summarily divide the common lands of a coparcenary estate between the different co-sharers. At present there is no law enabling revenue officers to change the constitution of a village from "imperfect pattidari" or "zamindari" to "pattidari," and yet it is certain that every Collector could give many examples, where the ruin of these village communities was solely or at any rate chiefly due to the quarrels which inevitably occur year

---

Valuable reports also of previous officers lie neglected in the record-room; a new Collector comes, and being quite ignorant of the district he is absolutely dependent on his Tahsildars; there may be within 20 yards of his desk careful and elaborate reports by his predecessors, but he knows naught of them, and it is no one's business to bring them to his notice; the revenue reports are brought up for disposal with all the other "mutafarrikat" (bundles of miscellaneous papers) by the sheristadar (head native clerk), whose only object is to get through them as quickly as possible. There is however in every Collector's office one person, whose services could be utilized with great advantage, and that is the District Kanungo; he is the proper person to bring up all the revenue reports, and it should be made his business to produce from the record office and to lay before the Collector all the previous reports bearing on the history and circumstances of the village in question.

Since this was written the N.-W. P. Government has issued orders for the more frequent employment of the Assistant Collectors in revenue business.

by year respecting the profits, or the management of the common lands.*

As the law now stands, the only partition allowed is that known as "perfect partition," the division, that is to say, of a village into two or three estates (mahals), each estate being henceforth responsible only for its own share of the Government revenue; it is the creation of many absolutely independent properties by a complete division of the whole area of the original unit between different members of the community.†

Under Act XIX of 1863 which lays down the procedure for the guidance of officers appointed to make such partitions, it is recorded that every co-sharer has a right to apply for the absolute separation of his own share; the creation of minute estates all paying their revenue separately to Government and not liable to any process on account of the default of another proprietor in the same village would however be a formidable evil. The Government revenue would be jeopardized and the work of the Collector would be seriously increased; it has therefore usually been the practice to refuse assent to any applications for division,

* As is remarked in the "Directions to Collectors," quarrels among the co-sharers are a fertile cause of default, yet no effort has been made to reduce the source of dispute. In "zamindari" villages it is most difficult for the co-sharer to obtain his quota of the profits; the patwari is the servant of the collecting headman, and he will give no clear accounts to the co-sharers; they have to blindly file a suit for a guess-sum, they must buy a stamped plaint, and incur other heavy expenses. As the Judicial Commissioner, Oudh, observed (para. 110, Oudh Civ. Rept., 1873), share-holders do not apparently know their powers of enforcing production of the village accounts from the patwari; claims for profits are frequently brought for round sums in excess of the proper amount on the avowed ground, that the plaintiffs have no means of ascertaining what is due to them.

† The law on the subject for the N.-W. P. is of course now contained in the Revenue Act of 1873, but this is with a few modifications merely a repetition of Act XIX of 1863. The Board of Revenue for the N.-W. P. remarks "on the usual delay and protraction in the execution of the troublesome class of cases" in their report for 1874.

if it appears, that the applicant's own share of the revenue is less than Rs 100.

The procedure laid down is so cumbrous and dilatory;* it places such numerous obstacles in the way of partition, that few proposed divisions are brought to a successful conclusion; the writer once made a vigorous attempt to see, in how short a time it was possible to effect a partition of a village into two separate estates (mahals), and, though not a single day was unnecessarily wasted, *nine months* elapsed before the partition received the assent of the Commissioner; it is notorious that in many cases after much annoyance and expense have been caused to the village co-sharers, and after

---

* It is scarcely necessary to give any illustration; when a petition for partition is presented, instead of the procedure being to summon all sharers, whose names are entered in the khewat, the first proceeding is the issue of a *notification* which according to the N.-W. P. Act runs for at least 30 days; within this time objections are to be filed; then according to Act XIX, after objections have been heard, a *proclamation* is issued to the effect, that the partition proceedings will be commenced on the expiry of another period of 30 days (Section 12) and so on.

An extract from the note appended to Section 116 of the N.-W. P. Revenue Act (in the edition by Messrs. Crosthwaite and Smeaton) will give some idea of the dilatoriness of the proceedings :—" The first step is to have the costs paid in; then all the parties should be summoned with the patwari and every particular of the mahal and of the existing tenure ascertained; a formal proceeding should then be drawn up laying down all the particulars of the partition, specifying the lands held in the mahal, the lands held in common, the lands held in severalty, &c., &c. In the course of this proceeding numerous disputes may arise, which will require to be settled, or overruled. The next step is to get the mahal surveyed. He will also test the rental filed by the patwari. If the settlement map is too antiquated for use, a new survey will be necessary,—the map is tested on the spot by some trustworthy officer. This having been done, &c., &c., &c., but it is not necessary to make further quotations; as the commentators observe, " at the best a partition is a long business, especially when some of the parties object to it, and throw every difficulty in the way."

Now for imperfect partition all that is required is an extract from the register (Khationi No. I) showing the common lands, and a copy of the khewat to give the share of each proprietor.

the proceedings have dragged their slow length along for 1½ and 2 years, the village is left undivided as before, since it is found impossible to fulfil all the conditions required by the Act.

In "imperfect pattidari" (partially divided) estates each co-sharer holds fields in every corner of the village; there is always one insuperable difficulty in the way of partition, *viz.* the impossibility of so dividing the village as to secure compactness of position for each new estate; in a word "chakbat" division (*i.e.*, division into blocks or compact tracts) cannot as a rule be effected, while the revenue authorities disapprove of "khetbat" division (*i.e.* division field by field) and usually refuse their assent to partitions effected on these terms. This is not an unreasonable objection, inasmuch as the assessment and collection of revenue for small "khetbat" estates is a very difficult matter; if an arrear occurs, direct collection by the Tahsildar would be a very objectionable process and few strangers would care to farm or purchase an estate, the fields of which lie mixed up with those of other estates held by ancestral landowners. Tenants are not easily procured and the settlement officer finds it almost impossible to satisfactorily fix the land-tax for these estates, if the fields be in every part of the township: it is most difficult to arrive at a just conclusion in regard to the capabilities of such estates.

No co-sharer can be compelled under the Act to surrender any field of his own share, so as to admit of partition in compact blocks, and in every village there are inevitably some landowners, such as the headmen, who are content with the existing constitution and who obstinately refuse to surrender any of the lands belonging to their share; the same difficulty is daily rendering the division of zamindari (undivided) estates an impossibility.

It is strongly urged, therefore, that the Collector should be authorized to depute one of his subordinates to divide the common lands of a "zamindari" (undivided) or of an "imperfect pattidari" (partially divided) village, and to apportion the revenue between the co-sharers (while still maintaining the joint responsibility as the "ultima ratio,") whenever it appears, either from his own inquiries or from the petitions of any co-sharers, that the interests of the Government and of the village community will be best served by a complete distribution of the village lands among the co-sharers in proportion to their shares; as each co-sharer would be allowed to retain his existing seer holdings, or in the case of imperfectly divided villages the tenant-leased lands already separately owned by him, the work of distribution would be very simple and very inexpensive; in fact the officer appointed for the purpose would merely have to inspect on the spot the common lands with the village rent-roll in his hand, and to then at once divide them among the co-sharers so as to give each that portion, to which his ancestral share entitled him; the Government land-tax would then be redistributed between the several sharers, and when a new register (Khationi No. 1) showing the lands belonging to each property had been prepared by the village accountant, the partition would be completed; the whole proceedings need not last four days. Section 134 of the North-West Provinces Revenue Act makes the consent of all the co-sharers necessary, and this proviso, it needs scarcely be remarked, effectually bars many required partitions; as has been pointed out there is usually one co-sharer at least, who is unwilling that the existing state of things should be altered, and, even if there were only two co-sharers the very reason for the petition of one would be the advantage gained by the other from the present constitution. It is difficult to understand, why the Government should take such care to allow perfect partition, which scarcely any one asks for, and should throw such obstacles in the way of imperfect partition, which is all really that most co-sharers desire: it is a great puzzle, why the consent of all the co-sharers should be thought necessary in order to divide fifty or hundred acres of common land, and why it should be considered unnecessary, when it is proposed to entirely sub-divide a village into several separate estates. It is much better for the Collector and for the settlement officer, that a village should not be partitioned off into separate minute estates; the revenue authorities will assuredly resist such proposals, and the result will be as before, that the involuntarily quarrelsome communities will continue to wrangle as of old.*

It may be argued, that it would be unjust to maintain the joint-responsibility, if each sharer thus obtains the absolute control over his share, but it must be recollected, that the complete partition of the village lands with a maintenance of the joint-liability of the whole proprietary body does not signify the creation of a new tenure; the tenure (pattidari) is already in existence, although it is comparatively rare. Moreover, it would be no injustice to hold all the sharers responsible only in the last resort for the default of one of their body, since they possess some very valuable privileges under this joint-tenure, even if they are unable to interfere in the management of one another's lands. They enjoy the right of escheat, and the right of pre-emption. They have a preferential claim to receive in transfer the share of a defaulter, and to the offer of the revenue-engagement, if their co-sharer refuses to accept the revised assessment.

As the law at present stands, it is impossible to effect the partition of under-proprietary holdings at all; yet

* As is observed in the "Directions to Collectors" (para. 170), the advantages of the imperfect partition are, that it holds the coparcenary community together, and thus promotes self-government; that it preserves to them the right of pre-emption conferred by Section 4, Act I, 1841, and that by decreasing the village expenses it enables them more economically to manage the estate. Its disadvantages are that by leaving the ultimate joint responsibility untouched, the industrious may suffer for the neglect of the idle members of the community, but this is obviated if the Collector never enforces the joint responsibility, until all measure to save realization of the land-tax from the defaulting pattidar have been tried.

these sub-holders, being far more embarrassed than the independent landowners, are still more likely to be constantly involved in disputes regarding the profits of the common lands. At this moment the writer has under disposal no less than between forty and fifty applications for the division of sub-settled holdings and of seer lands between the co-sharers, who admittedly are now fighting one another in regard to the collections and management, but no kind of partition can be carried out without the consent of all those interested, and, as before noted, it is found impossible to induce all the co-sharers to come to terms; there is urgent need therefore of the grant of full powers to the Collectors to compulsorily divide the common lands in such under-proprietary tenures.*

---

* This is especially required in Oudh, where there are in districts like Fyzabad and Gondah an immense number of sub-settled villages and seer holdings; these can never be divided under Act XIX, since they are included in the Talukdar's estate, which is of course not divisible into separate properties (mahals.)

For instance, 100 acres of land have been decreed to some Brahman under-proprietors; this plot only forms part of a village, and it is held on payment of the gross rental *minus* one-tenth; in the Nawabi the co-sharers left the management of the undivided property in the hands of one of their members; he is dead, and now they wish to have it divided between them, as they quarrel in regard to the management and profits, but nothing can be done; all will not consent to an amicable division, as the successor to the deceased manager prefers to act as sole rent collector.

Take for instance this case; B is a village decreed in birt to a resident under-proprietary body of Chaubes and Pandes; each family holds a half share of the property, but the lands are undivided; these Brahmans purchased the birt at different times from some Gahirwar Rajpoots, the original under-proprietors; in the Nawabi they quarrelled regarding the collections, and they still wrangle as of old; the Pandes asked for a division of the village into two equal shares, but the Chaubes, one of whom was the headman, refused to agree to a partition, and the proceedings had to be stayed; unless the law is altered these Pandes and Chaubes must go on fighting, until both they are ruined, and the Rajah is pressed to pay the land-tax due on this village; numbers of such instances could be given.

In making these proposals respecting the partition of common lands both in proprietary and under-proprietary estates, it is not intended that any repartition of already divided lands should be undertaken; in many estates held by proprietary and under-proprietary communities it is recorded as the village custom, that, if the estate be ever completely partitioned out among the co-sharers and any one co-sharer happen to hold more land than his share warrants, he shall receive a smaller portion of the common fields than the amount awarded to others; after the complete partition each should henceforth hold that amount of the total area of the estate, to which he is entitled according to his share; the settlement of a question like this will necessitate an inquiry into the proportionate area of each sharer's actual holding, but, as there is a clear record of the lands held by each co-sharer in the Khationi (No. I) the settlement of this question is not difficult; present possession would be taken at the basis of operations, and it would not be disturbed; the common lands would merely be partitioned out according to the share of each, so as to award to each sharer his due proportion of the total area of the original estate.

It has already been urged, that greater vigilance should be maintained over the Tahsildar's practical interpretation of the theory of the joint responsibility of all the recorded co-sharers of an estate, until the land-tax has been completely realized. The break-down of the "lumbardari" system, or in other words of the system under which the public business of these proprietary communities is managed by two or three headmen, whose office is hereditary, is, it is feared, only a question of time; we cannot expect, that, as they become accustomed to our mode of administration, and our code of jurisprudence, the co-sharers in these village communities will submit much longer to the dictation and supremacy of one or two of their body; those, who try to read aright the signs of the future, must admit that we cannot long hope to maintain the native system in its integrity.

Every effort should however be made to delay, as long as is practicable, the anticipated change, since the revenue business of the Collectors will necessarily increase in proportion to the separation of landed interests, and the sub-division of estates; in order therefore to render the present joint responsibility less burdensome and the system of representation by headmen more palatable than at present, not only should all the common lands be divided, when this is required, but each co-sharer should be allowed to pay in his quota of the revenue direct to the treasury, if he prefers to do so rather than to transmit the sum through his headman; as the headman would still be answerable in case of a summons from the Collector, and as he would still represent the community in all other public miscellaneous business, he should still receive the 5 per cent. remuneration for his services as the representative of the village.

Again, it is most advisable to prevent,* *as far as is possible,* the intrusion of strangers; when once a greedy money-lender, or a powerful neighbour has purchased or received in mortgage any share in an undivided or imperfectly divided estate, his arrival sows discord and dissension among the co-sharers; he probably collects by force all the rent of the common land, or at least a far larger portion, than the share which he holds would warrant, and the other proprietors strive in vain to make him refund. This more frequently occurs in under-proprietary communities; the proprietor has a grudge against the sub-holders; he

* Sir Charles Metcalfe's graphic description of the village communities has been often quoted, but this passage has not so frequently seen the light, and it is worth quotation:—"This union of the village communities," writes Sir Charles, "each one forming a separate little estate in itself, has, I conceive, contributed more than any other cause to the preservation of the people of India through all the revolutions and changes which they have suffered; and is on a high degree conducive to their happiness and to the enjoyment of a great portion of freedom and happiness. I wish, therefore, that the village constitutions may never be disturbed, and I dread everything which has a tendency to break them up."

bides his time and gets a decree against some defaulter; he succeeds in buying in the share of the debtor at the auction-sale; he enters into possession aided by a band of retainers, and he soon holds the under-proprietary body at his mercy. Sometimes a co-sharer has a grudge against his kinsmen and, to involve them in disputes with the superior owner, he sells his share to the latter.

The old Punjab Civil Code contained an excellent provision, whereby the right of pre-emption was "declared to exist in communities of landholders, however constituted, under whatever tenure the estate may be held;" no co-sharer could therefore sell his share to a stranger, until he had first offered it to the other members of the proprietary body, and to the hereditary cultivators, if there were any such resident on the estate.

This provision, however, does not go far enough; very few landowners sell their shares in the first instance; when they require ready money, they invariably resort to a usufructuary mortgage or supposed temporary transfer of their property; this mortgage is rarely redeemed, for the mortgagee obtains possession, and the profits of the estate are only considered as payment of the interest; unless the loan is repaid in a lump sum at a fixed date the mortgage becomes a sale; at any rate he holds possession of the share for many years. It is strongly urged, therefore, that no co-sharer should be allowed to transfer his share either by sale, or usufructuary mortgage to the hands of a stranger, until he has offered the share in sale or mortgage to the other members of the proprietary or under-proprietary body in succession according to the nearness of their relationship, and further, that at auction sales the co-sharers of any proprietary or under-proprietary body should have the right to secure the sold property on offering to pay the sum bid by the auction-purchaser.*

* Co-sharers in pattidari, *i.e.* divided estates alone, have the option of purchase at auction-sales under the present law, *vide* Section 14,

Further this right should also be allowed to sub-holders of all classes; the landowner should not be allowed to sell or mortgage to strangers, unless these birtias and other under-proprietors refused to buy or receive in mortgage the proprietary right of the landowner; *vice versâ* the landowner should be allowed the same privilege in cases where the whole, and not merely one or two, of the under-proprietary body desire to sell or mortgage their estate; it is most desirable, where it is possible, to get rid of these sub-infeudations, yet, as the law at present stands, the sub-holders will often to spite their landlord mortgage or sell their village to some stranger, although they know the former will give them a large sum for the transfer of their rights to him.

The difficulties experienced by the landowners in collecting their rents from the sub-holders of lands in their estates have been traced to the inapplicability of our system of law to this kind of tenure. Under the native government the landowner could always, under the strict law and custom of these tenures, cancel the lease given to the defaulting under-proprietor and collect the rents of the tenants through the agency of his own stewards and bailiffs;* he was not, therefore, as now, obliged to pay up

---

Act XXIII of 1861, but the section does not specify whether a nearer co-sharer has priority over a distant one in the event of both bidding; nor is any right of purchase given to under-proprietors, or to members of "imperfect pattidari" or "zamindari" estates.

* In revenue phraseology "as a rule, and by the custom of the country, the superior had the option of collecting the rental, either pakka or kacha" ("Lord Canning's Settlement of Oudh," p. 12), and as already pointed out in this respect the right of the Government over the landowner, and the right of the landowner over the under-proprietor were identical.

Our laws have, therefore, effected a great change in the relations of the two classes; the former rights of the superior owner in this respect have been summarily confiscated; formerly he could hold direct at pleasure; now he can never even seize the crops of a defaulting under-proprietor's seer, much less can he collect the rents from the latter's tenants.

to the Government officials the land-tax, assessed on his estate, before he had had time to collect the rents of his village. Under our system his only remedy, when the under-proprietors fail or refuse to pay, lies in a regular suit in the rent court to recover the arrears; this procedure entails great delays, and mulcts the suitor of large sums of money in the shape of court fees stamps, and lawyer's costs at the very time, when he is hard pressed to liquidate the revenue balances; moreover, as already shown, full satisfaction of a decree is rarely obtained, since the crops have in the interim been reaped and carried off.

As is indeed admitted by those who have paid any attention to these matters, we must in some degree return to the native revenue system in dealing with these under-proprietary difficulties. The rent demand due to the proprietor from each sub-holder must be first clearly specified and recorded in the settlement registers; to deal effectually with cases of default one of two courses must be adopted; either the superior owner must be allowed to exercise again his former power of collecting the rents himself by those coercive processes, which were at his disposal under the native government, or else the Collector must be authorized to employ against the under-proprietor those powers, which he already enjoys for the purpose of compulsory collecting the land revenue from the independent proprietors of landed estates.

It would obviously not be advisable in the interests of public peace to allow the landowners after this long interval (1856—1875) to arrest their under-proprietors, seize their moveable goods, to attach their crops, or to transfer and farm their shares; it is to be feared that such privileges would be now greatly abused to the imminent danger of constant riots and affrays, so bitter is the enmity which on many estates prevails between the two classes in consequence of the long litigation in our settlement courts.

It is not here suggested, that, as has been proposed, that the Collector should, on the application of the proprietor, be temporarily authorized to exercise his revenue coercive process against under-proprietary villages. Such a scheme would entail a most serious increase in the Collector's ordinary work in the shape of applications, enquiries, appointments of subordinate managers, arrangements for the collection of rents, compilation of new registers, in short all the worry and demoralization which results from temporary additions to routine business. The proprietor could not be allowed *suo motu* to hand over incorrigible defaulters to the Collector, or arbitrarily to select his own time for invoking that officer's aid, as, for instance, in a year of exceptional agricultural distress, or when perchance he had alienated, and half ruined them by extortion and harshness, and to retain the direct management and responsibility of collection and the more prosperous years; he would then only apply to the Collector, when he himself had found it impossible to make any collections, and when the crops had been carried off, in order to escape from his own liability to pay up the full land-tax; the efforts of his agent would be relaxed, and no doubt there would be constant disputes in regard to previous payments, which the overworked Collector, instead of the rent court, would have now to settle* in an executive capacity.

It is suggested that the revenue engagement for all sub-settled estates in which the holders of the sub-settlement were originally the independent landowners, and which were therefore included in the present superior owner's

* It is to be feared that the following extract would apply to many of these estates, if the Collector was suddenly called upon to take them in charge:—"They (the Superintendents of encumbered estates in Oudh) did not receive charge till June, and they succeeded not only to the mismanagement, which they were sent to remedy, but to bad harvests, an unknown staff, and unfamiliar duties; and they found in many cases the rents forestalled by the embarrassed owner before surrender of his management; allowances had to be punctually paid, which under the Talukdar would have been postponed to a more convenient day, and there were neither funds in hand, nor a banker to apply to, when the emergency had to be met."—Oudh Revenue Report, 1872, p. 18.

domains without any sale or mortgage, should be made with the under-proprietors; their estates should be registered as if they were independent villages (mufrid mahals), paying revenue direct to Government, and the Collector should for the future realize through the Tahsildar the total demand due from the estate; after the cost of management and the land-tax have been realized, the collections should be applied proportionately to the liquidation of the land-tax, and to the payment of the decreed percentage of the superior. It will probably be considered that the sanads granted to the Talukdars, bar this course, but the measure could be made conditional on their assent, and if they refused to assent, they should be left to realize the rents as at present, *i.e.* to certain loss and indebtedness. It is not improbable that a great many would prefer to hand over the villages to the Collector at least for the term of the present settlement. The Collector would of course exercise against the under-proprietors all the powers which he now possesses for the realization of the land-tax from the independent landowners; it is certain that this class of sub-holders would much prefer to pay in their rental at the Tahsil treasury than to the landowner's agent; the landowner would be permanently relieved of the burden of collecting rents from a number of discontented and disaffected sub-proprietary communities, and his receipt of his portion of the profits would be far more assured than it is at present. The Superintendents of the encumbered estates in Oudh could be specially authorized to exercise the Collector's revenue powers against all under-proprietors of the estates placed in their charge.

In regard to other under-proprietary estates, such as the birts referred to, it is proposed that the landowners should once for all, have the option of relinquishing the direct collection of the rent demand in favor of the Collector; if they assent to this change, the rental will be collected in the manner already described; if they refuse, the Collector should not be allowed the option of exercising in the future any revenue coercive powers unless the whole estate is placed in his charge from other causes, as in the case of wardship or the lunacy of the owner or when he holds it kurk or kham. It must be recollected, that in these estates, the sub-holders derived their title originally from the landowner's family, and, that they have always since the date of purchase been accustomed to hold their lands as his subordinates; they therefore have less reason to entertain those feelings of discontent or enmity towards their landlords which are inevitably excited in the case of sub-settled communities, whose villages were included in the larger estates of their neighbours* without their consent or under the pressure of a necessity, which no longer exists.

In all cases, while it would be dangerous to give the landowner any power to collect the rents direct from the cultivators, it would be advisable to amend the law of distraint, and to permit the attachment of the crops of any underproprietor's seer land for any failure in the payment of the rent; the settlement registers show the rent demand due from each co-sharer, where the land is divided, and the landowner might be permitted to attach under the law of distraint any under-proprietor's seer crops on the latter's

---

* According to Section 53 of the North-West Provinces Revenue Act, the settlement officer, guided by the rules framed by the Local Government, has power to determine, whether the superior landowner, or the under-proprietor shall be admitted to engage for the payment of the land revenue, due provision being made for securing the payment of the surplus profits to the superior holder.

As noted in the "Directions to Settlement Officers," "it has been the general rule in the North-West Provinces to make the settlement with the inferior proprietors, and this is the best arrangement when the superior and inferiors are unconnected by blood or clanship, and have been long opposed to each other, and the latter are clamorous for severance of interests. But where the two classes are of the same family or tribe and mutually willing to maintain their connection the former arrangement is very much the best."

Section 30 of the Punjab Revenue Act directs, that "when there are two classes of owners, superior and inferior, the settlement may be offered to either class, according as the Financial Commissioner directs."

default, whether that under-proprietor is a member of a large community or the single owner of small plot of decreed seer, sankallap, marwat, or other under-proprietary tenure.

In cases where the land is not divided, the total arrears of rent could, in accordance with the universal village custom be distributed rateably over the shares of the different under-proprietors, and their seer crops could, on their refusal to pay their share, be distrained; if the headman should be found guilty of embezzlement, or gross negligence, he could be deposed, and another co-sharer could be selected to fill his place if he failed to present his due quota. The Collector has already, under the Oudh Rent Act (Section 125), power to farm or transfer any share of a defaulting under-proprietor on his failure to satisfy any rent decree, if it appears that the satisfaction of the decree together with a fair interest can be obtained in a reasonable period by either of those methods; the sale of an under-proprietary right is not allowed, unless the Collector has signified, that satisfaction of the decree cannot be obtained without resorting to this extreme measure.

It will be no breach of official confidence, if it is asserted that at the present time every Superintendent of encumbered estates in Oudh is pressing urgently for sanction to the sale of various under-proprietary tenures as the sole means of realizing the arrears of rent owed by many of these recusant or insolvent sub-holders. In many cases the estate is so hopelessly involved in debt, or the under-proprietors are so stubbornly resolved to remain in arrears, that no measure, save the stern application of this *ultima ratio*, will either satisfy the outstanding decrees, or cow the rest of the under-proprietary body into a punctual discharge of their rent-demand.

Yet Mr. Crosthwaite and the other writers, who hold his views, condemn severely the compulsory sale of ancestral property in land either by the courts in execution of a civil or rent decree, or by the owner himself in the shape of a voluntary transfer. It is urged that the State should once for all abandon its rights to sell estates as a coercive process to secure the realization of the land-tax, and it is further proposed, that the Government of India should be endowed with a legal right of pre-emption to all land. To give the proposal in Mr. Crosthwaite's own words, the details of the measure might be something as follows :— "No sale of any land direct or conditional, or by decree " of court should be made unless an offer of the land had " first been made to the Government, and declined by it; " a certain percentage of profit should be laid down, say " ten per cent., and, unless a careful valuation of the estate " showed that the rental would yield that profit, the Gov- " ernment should in ordinary cases refuse to buy, or " become owner of the estate. There would be several courses " open to pursue. If the outgoing proprietors were men " of family and influence, or if there was any special reason " for wishing to maintain them, it would be easy to make " a settlement with them on terms sufficient to yield the " required amount of profit. If the outgoing proprietor " had himself purchased the estate or were a man of bad " character, or one whom it was thought better to be rid of, " a settlement could always be made on very advantageous " terms with the hereditary tenants. If neither of these " courses could be approved, the estate could be held under " the direct management of the Collector, or farmed to one " of the best landlords in the neighbourhood. In estates " thus purchased by Government, there would remain to " the ex-proprietors, no matter, whether the estate was set- " tled with them or not, no proprietary right which they " could again pledge, or transfer." They would however under this scheme retain their seer at fixed favorable rates.

The supposition appears to be that land did not change hands under native governments, and that therefore we should not allow it to be permanently alienated, for Mr.

Crosthwaite writes, that hand in hand with the undoubted benefits of our rule "came another innovation, that has gone far in the eyes of the people to nullify all, that they have gained. I refer to the forced sale of land for debt, or in arrears of revenue." This is however a total mistake; compulsory sale of the property of defaulting revenue-payers either to their sureties, or to strangers, was not an unusual practice of native government; when it was shown, that the defaulter was unable to pay up the current revenue demand, the Revenue Collector frequently arrested him, and refused to release him, till he raised the required sum by sale or mortgage;* similarly a landowner, who was hopelessly involved in debt would often transfer his estate or share by voluntary mortgage or sale.†

* Not only did the native officials on this indirect way force defaulters to sell or mortgage their property, but in some cases the Government directly sold an estate for arrears of revenue; as the Oudh Chief Commissioner wrote in 1866:—"Sales of land in discharge of arrears of revenue were prevalent on Bengal and Behar under the native rule; they were called by-i.-sultanee, or sales on account of the Emperor, and they are appealed to by Mr. Shore in Appendix 14 at p. 306 of Harington's Analysis as proof of private property in the soil. There are instances of such sales under the same designation in the Oudh district." For instance, Rajah Krishan Dat Ram purchased in 1259 F.S. the Bangaon estate of Gya Pershad, Sadr Kanungo of Gondah, when it was sold for arrears of revenue.

† Here, for instance, is the traditional history of a village; it belonged originally to some Ahirs; they are said to have sold it to some Syads, who sold it to one Udwat S.; he transferred it to a Sheikh neighbour who in his turn mortgaged it to the Kanungo of the pargana; the latter finally sold it to some Janwars, and they obtained a decree for the proprietary right in the settlement courts.

Take another village; in 1835 A.D., one sharer named Subah S. fell into debt and absconded; the rest of the co-owners paid up the arrears of revenue, and divided the share of the defaulter; subsequently another sharer, Hurde S., mortgaged half his ancestral share and also his portion of Sukha's lands to a relative living in a neighbouring village; on Hurde's death his widow mortgaged the other half to a Paonwar relative, who in his turn mortgaged it to a co-sharer of Hurde S.

There is scarcely an Oudh village, in which, prior to annexation, some share or other had not been voluntarily sold or mortgaged by one co-sharer to another; it is true that the small local money-lenders rarely bought or received in mortgage such shares, because the other members of the proprietary, or under-proprietary body would not have allowed the usurer to take possession of any portion of the village lands, nor indeed was the former bold enough to undertake the responsibility in those days, when blows were freely dealt; under native rule security from violence depended on the strength of a man's arm, the fearlessness of his character and the number of his kinsmen and not on a police force or on a Magistrate's energy. Similarly when a village proprietary body found it impossible to pay off the heavy balances of land revenue, and were too weak to resist the Revenue Collector, or too peaceable to fly to the jungles and take up the trade of robbers, they sold or mortgaged their estates to their surety, to a neighbour, to the Government revenue farmer, or to a powerful Rajah; as already remarked, the effect of such a transfer was often very transient; the mortgagee or purchaser might die, might be disgraced, might himself fall into arrears, and be dispossessed, and in due time the ancestral owners would regain possession of their property unshackled by any back debts, or revenue balances.

In 1203 F.S., some co-sharers mortgaged their lands to a Gahirwar neighbour; in 1244 F., his family mortgaged the same property to some Sukal cultivators, who have obtained a decree in our courts. Burrear, S.'s widow, on her husband's death, gave over her share to a cousin; he mortgaged it to Dhar S. of another village, and the latter sold to a co-sharer of Burrear S.

Utravan was a village belonging to some Janwars, but they fell into arrears in 1243 F.; the chukladar arrested them and shut them up in his lock-up; after a time they agreed to raise the required sum by a sale of their estate, and they signed a deed of sale in favor of a Lucknow resident, who paid Rs. 3,000 for the property; the old zamindars received a yearly allowance of Rs. 175 as nankar.

Under these circumstances there can be no good reason, why under our rule a bankrupt's landed estate should not be held liable for his debts, as much as and to the same extent as his other property. A prohibition of the sale of landed property now would merely act as a premium on extravagance; there is no object to be gained by retaining in possession of their lands men who have only their own profligate habits to thank for their fall, or men, who are so hopelessly ruined, that there is no prospect of their return to a state of solvency; as a punishment for wilful mismanagement and wanton extravagance it is to be hoped that the power of sale vested in the Government will always be promptly and vigorously exercised; of recent years Local Administrations are pleased to note in their annual reports that no estate has been sold by Government orders for arrears of revenue, while their subordinates could count up by scores the villages, which the owners have been forced to sell privately solely owing to the unyielding severity of the Government system of assessment and collection. Let the land-tax be equitably assessed and nothing can have a more salutary effect than the prompt punishment of a wilful defaulter by the public sale of his estate: if a land-owner refuses to pay a reasonable land-tax, he is not entitled to receive any consideration; at present Government officers dislike proposing sale because they have misgivings whether the tax-payer or the Government is the real culprit.

Mr. Crosthwaite does not state, who is to decide the amount of the purchase-money to be paid by the State; if the market value is to be offered, that would in many cases operate as a bar to purchase by the State, for the profit of the estate would not give the required percentage. In many neighbourhoods land fetches a fancy price, irrespective of its paying-value in hard cash, as it does in the home counties of England; if the vendor is not to be allowed to obtain the full possible purchase-money, he will be a direct loser by this scheme, while, if he is to secure as much as he can get in open market, the State will frequently be obliged to decline a costly and profitless purchase; in the purchase of land sentiment and other considerations than the mere money-value of the property frequently enhance the market price; a co-sharer would, for instance, offer a far higher sum for his kinsman's estate than a mere stranger, or the Government could afford to give, for purchase by an outsider must be regarded as a mere commercial enterprise.

Conceive too the amount of extra work, which will be inevitably thrown upon the shoulders of the unfortunate Collector; landed property will under any system change hands with some frequency, especially where there is great sub-division of estates, and every case of contemplated transfer will in future develop into a "misl" (or set of official papers) for the Collector's detectation; every intending seller will have to apply to that officer on a stamped petition; there will be endless inquiries by subordinate officers, elaborate estimates of the value of the land in question will have to be prepared, and the staff of officials will have to be increased in every district. It would be simply impossible for the Collector to superintend the execution of this scheme.

If the Collector, after elaborate enquiry, came to the conclusion that the State might without risk undertake the venture and buy the offered estate, of course reports to and the sanction of his superior officers would be necessary. But he could never propose purchase until he had satisfied himself, that he could either farm the estate, settle it with some cultivators, or satisfactorily manage it himself; even if satisfied on these points, he would have also to ascertain the seer area and fix the rent to be paid for this land by the ex-proprietors; he would further have to discover and record the manorial rights, which the dispossessed owner is to henceforth enjoy.

In many cases it will appear, that nearly all the land in the village is cultivated by the landowners; the profits of the estate will therefore be very small, and the management will be very difficult. Under this scheme the State would in a very short time have sunk an immense capital in the purchase of estates, which from the very fact of their sale by the ancestral owners, have plainly proved from some cause or other to be unprofitable properties; such investments would be very dangerous even for an energetic resident landlord, and would signify a still more riskful enterprise to an impersonal absentee owner, as the Government would necessarily be. It is to be feared that the returns would scarcely justify an undertaking of this magnitude.

The practical difficulties in the way of this scheme have been overlooked; presumably its advocate has for years been engaged in other work, than the business of collecting land revenue; there can be little doubt that every Collector in the service would shrink appalled from such a project; in many cases it would be simply impossible to settle the estate with either resident cultivators or strangers, and it would be equally impracticable, to manage it direct; if the power to sell is taken away, there will be no security left for the realization of the revenue.*

* To give an instance.—There was a large estate of some 16 villages owned in sub-settlement to the neighbouring Rajah by a single member of a Bisscin clan:—the owner was a man of lazy, profligate and improvident character; he never paid the slightest attention to the management of his estate, to the collection of the rent, or to the liquidation of the rent-demand due to the superior owner; he spent large sums in excess of his income, and to retrieve his fortunes, or to secure sums of ready money, he from time to time sold birt rights in fractions of his villages to resident cultivators, or to some tenants, who lived in villages just over the borders of another province.

The land-tax, on the basis of which his rent-demand was fixed, was moderate, for it was carefully revised, and not a hundred rupees were reduced on his whole estate; his annual rent amounted to some Rs. 3,300; in one year he paid but Rs. 192 to the Rajah, yet the latter

It would seem absurd to purchase the estate and then resettle it with the sold-up ex-owner, for he has shown himself already incompetent to undertake its management; if his embarrassments are due to over-assessment, or bad seasons, he is of course entitled to relief in the shape of a reduction in the land-tax, or a remission of arrears ; it is only in cases, when the landowner is reduced to offer sale owing to his own mismanagement, that the Collector would be unable to propose relief.

It might be supposed, that farm or transfer would be in all cases an easy process, but practical acquaintance with a Collector's work would lead most thinkers to the conclusion, that in many cases it is impossible to secure any one willing to take the estate, especially if the new-comer has to pay not only the revenue demand, the costs of future litigation, the wages of the village accountant and watchmen and the heavy cesses, but also the 10 per cent. due to the State as its return on the purchase-money, and further he would find the assets of the property most seriously reduced by the grant of seer to the ex-proprietors at a rate equal to only three-fourths of the possible

---

had to pay the land-tax, some Rs. 2,000, to the Collector; so things went on from bad to worse; the cultivators and birtias did what they liked and rarely paid their rent in full, while the owner continued to sell plots of land to his tenants in order to defray pressing demands; in some four or five years the Rajah had obtained decrees for sums exceeding Rs. 13,000 on account of unpaid rent, and the Collector took the estate into his direct management; it was found however that satisfaction of the decrees could not possibly be obtained in this way, since the Collector had no time to exercise any personal control over the paid manager; the birtias, when pressed for their rents, absconded across the border, while the cultivators were all of high-caste, and were regular defaulters. No one would take the estate on farm; it was not worth the trouble, and no solvent cultivators could be found to undertake the management of the villages, so sale was inevitable, and the property was bought by a banker, who could afford the speculation. The sale was a proper punishment for the owner's reckless behaviour, and it proved a salutary warning to his neighbours.

rental;* it is clear, that the profits would not repay him for the trouble of management, and for the risk of failure to pay the land-revenue in full.

No one would take in farm a village full of these ex-proprietors, who are so graphically described by Mr. Colvin as ready to break the head of the intruding stranger, and as steadily refusing to pay their rents to the new landlord; it is not likely also that any person, however bold in his commercial undertakings, will come forward to take charge of an estate tenanted by high caste cultivators, who rarely pay their old landlords in full and who would simply laugh at the efforts of a new comer to collect rent. As for the cultivators themselves, in many cases, they are either high-caste tenants, who are regular defaulters or low-caste men, who have no influence whatever, and who would be quite unable to manage the village in the presence of the ex-proprietor, or to obtain a farthing of rent from the latter for his seer fields. The change from serf to master would be too sudden. It is not often that a cultivator of the required stamp could be procured, a man, that is, of adequate means and also of sufficient influence who could give some security to the Collector for the due payment of the land-revenue.

It cannot be doubted that this scheme would result in the utter demoralization of the landowning classes; secure against complete dispossession as he would be under this proposal, since he is to retain his seer and his manorial dues, and with the prospect of being restored to his estate under the operation of Mr. Crosthwaite's sinking fund,†

---

* Take for example Mauza S—; out of a cultivated area of 253 bighas no less than 237 bighas are cultivated by the landowners in their seer; or K--where the owners till 269 bighas as opposed to 363 bighas rented to resident tenants.

† "It should be a part of the scheme, that when the estate was resettled with the ex-proprietors, any payment that they might agree to make, over and above the minimum profit required should form a sinking fund to repay the Government to lay back the full proprietary right in the land."—P. 229, Calcutta Review, No. CXII.

what motive will he have now for economy and thrift? Assuredly, the answer must be that this scheme would increase his recklessness, strengthen his improvidence, diminish his energy, intensify his profligacy and plunge him deeper and deeper into debts and difficulties; it would undoubtedly act as an incentive to extravagance, and it would contribute most vigorously to the earlier ruin of the classes, whom its proposers seek to aid.

It is said that, by refusing to sell land in execution of decrees, we shall diminish the security available for the money-lenders, and thereby render them more careful in their money-loans, that landowners finding it ever more difficult to obtain a supply on their personal security, will become more provident, and that, in fact the prohibition of the sale of property in land will act as a regenerator of the landed classes. To arguments of this kind the answer is easy, that all experience shows, that men without money will borrow, and that money-lenders will lend, however harsh the law against usury may be, or however fragile may be the security offered, that the only effect of a law prohibiting the sale of land would be to raise the rate of interest to a height, which would in the money-lender's opinion compensate him for the greater risk, and that such a law would merely render the fall of the improvident landowner more speedy and more complete. For it is admitted, that money-lenders are possessed by an intense desire to obtain possession of landed property under our rule, and it is not improbable, that, if it is rendered impossible for them to acquire such estates, they will raise the rate of interest, for in many cases that rate is fixed at a lower figure, than otherwise might have been secured, in the very hope of obtaining the estate at the expiry of the term named in the deed.

The disadvantages of direct management have already been indicated, and it is not necessary to refer to them again. It is clear, moreover, that the scheme could not be applied to the sales of small shares in villages or of seer holdings, birts, maáfis, sankallaps, marwats, and the various under-proprietary tenures of districts, like those of Gondah and Fyzabad in Oudh ; it would be impossible for the State to purchase these minute properties, or to secure their effective management after purchase.

The strongest objection against this scheme is however this, that it is not wanted; the Collector has in all cases of revenue arrears the power with the sanction of his superiors to transfer or farm or hold direct any estate or share, and it is strongly recommended, that he should carry out these coercive processes in all possible cases; similarly the civil and rent courts can always under Sections 243 and 244 of the Procedure Code resort to a temporary alienation of this nature, if it appears, that the debt can be thus realized within a reasonable period.* These sections could indeed be made more stringent, and it could be provided that the Court should not wait for the judgment-debtor's application, as is prescribed, but that it should refuse to sanction sale, until it appeared that no other scheme could secure the satisfaction of the decree. The provisions of the Oudh Rent Act contained in Sections 124 and 125 could be introduced into the N.-W. P.† and also, if necessary, the rule which requires the sanction of the highest judicial authority to the sale of ancestral properties in land.

The N.-W. P. Rent Act of 1873 has secured to any person, who may in the future lose or part with his

* The N.-W. P. Rent Act (Section 174) gives 15 years with interest at 6 per cent. as the reasonable period within which the decree must be realized.

† Section 173 of the N.-W. P. Rent Act only applies to the sale of a mahal or share of a mahal belonging to a person who holds land as a tenant in another estate, in execution of a decree for rent due for the cultivation in that estate; it does not apply to the sale of an under-proprietor's land in satisfaction of a rent decree on account of such land.

proprietary rights in any estate, a right of occupancy in the lands held by him as his seer at the date of the loss of the estate, and he is entitled to hold this land at a rent, which is to be four annas in the rupee less than the prevailing rate payable by tenants-at-will for land of similar quality, and with similar advantages; these privileged cultivators are to be termed ex-proprietary tenants.

This provision is no doubt a wise and statesman-like method of securing some protection for the dispossessed landowner of the N.-W. Provinces; there is however as yet no law securing any similar privileges for dispossessed proprietors in Oudh, the Punjab, or the Central Provinces, and a measure of this nature is urgently required in Oudh, for in a short while it is to be feared, that our revised assessments and our system of administration will have succeeded in compelling numbers of landed proprietors to effect a sale or mortgage of their estates.

On this point there seems to have been some misapprehension, on the part of some members of the legislative council; according to the official report of the speeches delivered on the 21st November 1873, Mr. Inglis remarked that in proposing the grant of these privileges to the ex-proprietor "we were doing no more than following the " example already set us by the Punjab and Oudh, the two " provinces close to us, where the tenure under which land " is held resembles ours most closely."* In Oudh no more has been done than to maintain the *statu quo* by decreeing to ex-proprietors their seer lands in all cases, when it can be shown, that in the Nawabi they did hold these lands at favorable rates. It is a mistake to suppose, that under the native government all dis-

* Sir W. Muir also said that "had the principle of the Oudh settle- " ment been followed from the first, the ruin of the ex-proprietors would " have been avoided; and we should have been saved from a vast " amount of the agrarian dangers, which threatened us in the mutiny " and the troublous times that followed."

possessed or sold up landowners retained their cultivation at low rates; in many cases where, for instance, the sale was a *bonâ fide* one, and full consideration was received, they did not in fact retain any privileges of this nature; they were reduced to the level of mere tenants-at-will, and they paid rents at the same rates, as those exacted from ordinary cultivators. It was to secure some privileges for this class of ex-proprietors, that the much discussed fifth section of the Oudh Rent Act was passed; this provided that those dispossessed landowners, who could not show that they have ever cultivated lands at favorable rates since the loss of their estate, but who had retained possession of their property up to within thirty years of annexation, were allowed under this section a right of occupancy in all fields which were in their cultivating occupancy on the 24th July 1865, provided that they had held them as tenants in some year prior to annexation.

Seer, as a privileged holding, means a holding at favorable rates, and in Oudh all ex-proprietors who could show that they held lands at favorable rates within the twelve years preceding 1856 A.D. have secured decrees for under-proprietary right in such fields at the rates paid prior to annexation; they have full power of sale, mortgage or gift in regard to their sub-holdings, or, as it worded, they have a heritable and transferable right, whereas the occupancy tenants of the Rent Act have only a heritable, and not a transferable, right. The word "seer," as commonly used in some districts, signifies merely a tenant's own cultivation, land, that is to say, which he tills with his own plough and bullocks as distinct from the fields which he sub-lets to another cultivator. In Gondah, for instance, all classes of tenants, both ex-proprietors, birtias, who were always sub-holders, lessees, and high-caste or even low-caste tenants, talk familiarly of their "seer," and these latter cultivators by no means imply that they claim any rights in regard to this holding either in the shape of low rent, or of exemption from liability to ejectment.

The settlement courts could only decree these under-proprietary rights on the basis of possession within the twelve years preceding annexation, which was the special period of limitation provided by law for the hearing of all suits for titles in land; at the closing of the settlement courts, however, the ordinary period of limitation comes into operation, and claimants, who have been dispossessed for more than twelve years from the present date, cannot now bring any suit to recover possession.

The occupancy clauses of the Oudh Rent Act only apply to those ex-proprietors who sold or parted with their proprietary right prior to annexation; under the present law, therefore, there is no provision whatever for securing any privileges to those proprietors in Oudh who shall in the future have to part with their estate, or who have already been compelled to sell their property between the closing of the settlement operations, and the present date; unless they reserve to themselves their seer lands in the deed of sale, or unless the Judicial Commissioner in the case of auction-sales secures them this privilege, they become mere tenants-at-will.

In regard to the proposed Bankruptcy Courts it is clear that they would in no way remedy the evils here described; the object of Government is to save the landowners from the necessity of parting with their hereditary estates; if once they have lost their property, a white-wash in an insolvency court will avail them little; all the property of an applicant for the liquidation of his affairs must be sold before he can receive his discharge.

It has been frequently proposed to enact laws for the repression of usury by fixing a maximum rate of interest which can be recovered in the law courts; those who have made a proposal of this kind have however omitted to face all the difficulties which stand in the way of the introduction of such a measure. No objection can be urged against this proposal on the ground of "interference with power of free contract" or for such like reasons drawn from politico-economical theories in favor with the rulers of European states; oriental countries differ widely from civilized states, and European principles of legislation and of "laissez faire" are completely misplaced in India; in truth there can be no free contract between the ignorant landowners of this country and a strong guild of greedy usurers who possess a complete monopoly of money-lending.

The success of the scheme is doubtful for other reasons than these; in the first place it would be necessary to frame tables of permissive rates; 33 per cent. may be a low rate of interest for a ruined land proprietor, or an indebted cultivator, while 24 per cent. would be an excessive demand from a landowner whose estates were unburdened by a single encumbrance; it would clearly not be sufficient to enact that no one should pay above a certain rate, for there are many cases where the borrower is so hopelessly in debt that the money-lender would be justified in demanding 50 per cent. for his risk; if laws against usury are introduced, the courts must treat each case on its merits, and decide whether the interest exacted was fair or excessive; it would however be very dangerous to entrust the courts with such extensive power; in every suit for the recovery of loans long inquiries would be necessary in respect to the borrower's means of payment at the date of his receipt of the loan; the court would have to determine whether 33 per cent., 50 per cent., 24 per cent., 18 per cent., or 12 per cent. should be considered the proper rate for the trader, the coolie, the landowner, or the artisan; such jurisdiction would give rise to endless litigation, to dishonesty on the part of debtors, and to a general tendency towards breach of contract, while it would excite feelings of distrust and suspicion in the minds of the money-lenders. What would be the consequence? It seems incredible to suppose that the courts will be able to satisfactorily decide nice questions concerning the proper rates of interest in each suit; the money-lenders will as often unjustly suffer as the borrowers, and they will naturally protect their own interests by more systematically adhering to a practice not now in any way unknown, namely, the retention of part of the loan itself as security for or as prepayment of the stipulated interest; as the consideration is all stated in the bond to have been received, the borrower cannot plead in court that he has not as a fact received all the principal, and he will therefore as before be paying the same or a more usurious interest; the money-lender will also doubtless resort more regularly to the practice of compelling their creditors to sign fresh bonds, in which the *unpaid interest* calculated frequently at compound rates and all the unpaid capital are entered as representing the principal only of a fresh loan.

It is not to be doubted also that the money-lenders would under such a law refuse to lend on mere money-bonds; they would demand mortgage deeds, and we should more frequently than ever see stipulations providing that the money-lender is to have possession of the borrower's estate, and that the profits are only to be credited in lieu of the interest; such profits would in many cases represent the usurious interest which the law has forbidden, yet, it is difficult to see how the courts can be allowed to interfere with written and registered contracts of this special nature without assuming a general power to adjudicate upon the conditions of all written contracts whatsoever.

It is to be feared that it is impossible to do more to protect the borrowing classes from the money-lenders than to allow the law courts a general power to refuse decrees for interest when it appears from the evidence that it is grossly excessive; if for instance a money-lender sues a landowner for interest at 50 per cent., and then it appears that the landowner is in full possession of his estate, the courts should refuse, as is the practice in the Punjab, to decree interest at this excessive rate; these are, it is to be feared, only isolated cases, it is the 24 per cent., and the 33 per cent., supplemented by fresh bonds or mortgage deeds, which cripple most borrowers.

The courts can apply other remedies to check undue rapacity on the part of the usurers; easy instalments at reasonable interest can be fixed for the payment of the decree; compound interest can be rigidly refused; in the absence of proof of special agreement with the borrower, the court can and should refuse to allow interest above 6 per cent. or 12 per cent., or in special cases any interest at all for the time which has elapsed between the falling due of the sum now claimed, and the date of the institution of the suit; this would compel money-lenders to at once sue their creditors, and would prevent them from deliberately waiting, until the debt had risen to a sum, which the borrower is only able to pay by an auction-sale of his whole property; the court can also refuse to allow interest on the sum decreed for the interval which may elapse between the date of the decree and the date of realization.

Can any means now be adopted to find any sources of employment for the vast and ever-increasing numbers of the small proprietary and under-proprietary communities of Oudh? It is not fair to charge the members of the Rajpoot clans with habits of profligacy, because their numbers increase; they marry in early life, and they all marry, because marriage is a quasi-sacred ordinance, inculcated, from their earliest childhood, as the main object of life, and, even in the matter of progeny, there is no reason to suppose, that these early marriages result in the birth of an inordinate number of children for each family. As Doctor Thornton writes:—"The procreation of children ranks as highly among religious duties as their baptism does in Europe, and its neglect is held to be punishable with equally awful penalties;" but his remarks are only true in regard to the supposed religious necessity for the birth of a son and heir; as he rightly proceeds to add:—"Where to die without leaving behind a son to perform one's general obsequies is supposed to be almost equivalent to signing a warrant of eternal self-damnation, imprudence is naturally of small account, and all possible precautions are as naturally taken against childlessness."

The young Rajpoot does find some employment in the police (but that is limited source of service) and also in the ranks of the army of chaprasis (official personal attendants like commissionaires) who swarm in the various public offices, but the great majority, destitute of any incentive to exertion, and ignorant of any opening in life, idle away their lives at the door of their homes, or under the shade of the village fig tree, as purely unproductive consumers, whose existence means ruin and beggary to the village community. Yet it must not be supposed, that the Rajpoot is an effiminate idler; he has made, and always would make, a fine soldier, but the ranks of the native army have been greatly reduced since the mutiny, and a soldier's life is now a dull routine of drills, pipe-clay and musketry practice. It is impossible not to like the Rajpoot clansman, well described* as "manly and frank, proud of his birth and lineage, and of his old profession of fighting. His face is generally handsome, and his physique good. He will eat meat, when he can get it, and sometimes it is a boast with such a one, that he never eats without meat. His dress is a *dhoti* and *mirzai*, or light thin jacket and a light cap, and gold earrings will complete his costume. Thus clad, and armed with a bamboo staff, which has been rubbed to a polish, he will talk to you, and beat up game for you for hours."

Emigration is not for these yeomen, since they are too proud to handle the plough; the cultivation of waste lands, and the establishment of new hamlets is fit work for the Ahir and the Lodh, the industrious tillers of the soil, but not in their estimation for the descendants of a long line of warrior forefathers, and to a certain extent Englisnmen can understand the feeling. The prospect is indeed a distressing one, and it would seem, that, bearing in mind the large revenue, which Oudh contributes to swell the imperial budget, the establishment of an Oudh

* Mr. Butts' Lucknow Settlement Report, p. 59.

local force, or of an Oudh militia constitutes, as has been suggested, the sole resource for the amelioration of the circumstances and prospects of the Rajpoot clansmen of that province.*

It may be well here to note, how our system of assessment affects the tenantry of the assessed estates. If the land-tax is based on the actual rental of a village, there is no reason why the condition of the tenant should be affected injuriously, save so far as a heavy enhancement, at once levied from the landholder without any period of respite, obliges him to try to recoup himself for his decreased income by a general enhancement of rents.

In other cases, however, the action of the settlement department must press heavily on the cultivators, as for instance in the Meerut district, where the rents had apparently remained stationary for nearly thirty years, yet the new settlement raised the tax 88 per cent. at once and abandoned the cultivators to the tender mercies of the rent courts by virtually admonishing the landowners to effect an enhancement of rent up to this percentage.

Again, in many instances, the settlement officer appears to have endeavoured to commute all grain rents into

---

* The policy of spending some part at least of the Oudh surplus revenues in Oudh for the advantage of its inhabitants was one strenuously urged by both Sir W. Sleeman and Sir Henry Lawrence. The latter wrote in 1856:—"My paper on Oudh would serve as a guide to present doings in all points save the disposal of the surplus revenue, which assuredly ought to be spent *in Oudh*. Nor indeed do I think, that we should materially lose, or fail to gain thereby. Is it nothing, that we should make a garden of the nursery of our sepoys, and open out the resources of a province bordering for a thousand miles on our old ones?" This passage is quoted on p. 454 of Kay'e Sepoy War, Vol. I.

Sir W. Sleeman is as explicit:—"I shall recommend that all establishment, military, civil, and fiscal, be kept entirely separate from those of our own Government, that there be no mistake as to disinterestedness of our intention towards Oudh," but there is no necessity to quote his words, as his views on the Oudh annexation question are well known.

cash rents, whether the cultivators were willing to pay cash rents, or whether they wished to continue their grain payments;* in villages, where the crops are specially exposed to drought, flood, or to the ravage of wild beasts, and where therefore the produce of the fields is very uncertain and fluctuating, the tenants regard a grain rent as their sole protection, as they only till such land in favorable years, and they then have merely to pay to their landlord one-half, one-third, one-fourth, one-fifth of the actual crop;† they at any rate have not to pay rent, when their fields have not produced a crop; as is the outturn, so are their payments to the landlord, and bad seasons or other agricultural disasters only affect them, so far as the portion of the crop obtained by themselves is thereby rendered scanty and insufficient. If the grain-rent is converted compulsorily into a fixed cash-payment, they are liable for the rent, whether the fields yield a good outturn, or in fact lie fallow. In other districts immemorial custom has, as it were, sanctified the payment of grain-rent, and the cultivators knowing that under this system there is no rack-renting, prefer it to a régime of cash payments, which bring in their train the rent court and the decree.

---

* Cf. the reports of the Collectors of Aligarh, Furruckabad, and Moradabad in the Board of Revenue Report for 1874, N.-W. P., p. 54, *passim.*

For instance, the Commissioner of Rohilkhond points out that "there is much ill-feeling throughout the Moradabad district just now between landlords and tenants. This is mainly attributed to the antagonism of interest which is being brought out by the present settlement, especially by the commutation into money of rents in kind."

† The landholders in this country never exact more than half the outturn of each field, so the cultivators, who till their lands on grain-rents are better off, than the tenants-at will in Southern Italy, where the peasant's share is generally a third, often only a fourth, and is even sometimes reduced to a sixth part of the produce of the land he tills. While the cultivator is mulcted of this large share of the crop, he is nevertheless expected to provide the seed, the oxen, and the instruments of husbandry.

It is unwise to interfere between the cultivator and the landlord in these cases; the action of the settlement department in its endeavours to place the relations of the tenant and the proprietor, on what, it fancies, to be a more satisfactory footing, is likely to create much discontent, distrust, and ill-feeling. On this point the wishes of the Government of India were clearly indicated in 1832; it is recorded that "His Lordship entirely concurs with the Sudder Board in thinking, that any arbitrary determination by the officers of Government of the sums payable as rent may be extremely mischievous, specially where a payment in kind is converted into a money payment; and His Lordship is further of opinion, that, should they believe the practice to be prevalent, it will be the duty of the Sudder Board to lose no time in circulating such instructions, as may be calculated to suppress that practice, without diminishing the encouragement to be afforded to the voluntary issue of pottahs."

Following the example of two native landholders, the Government manager of a large estate in Oudh used to hold a yearly assembly of his chief lessees and cultivators, for the purpose of presenting cheap presents, such as a shawl, a head-dress, &c., to those of his dependents, who had paid up their rents in full: a kind word accompanied each small present, and the gifts were highly valued; the act showed at any rate, that the manager endeavoured to maintain friendly relations with his best tenants. This practice obtains also in the Opium department and bears the happiest fruit, yet the Collector of the land-tax neither knows personally, nor bestow any mark of approval upon those landholders in his district, who faithfully discharge their obligations to the State. It is suggested, that the Collectors of districts should follow the excellent example of the opium officers and hold annual durbars for the presentation of small rewards to the respectable and punctual payers of revenue. The argument, that they would thereby be lowering the high dignity of their office is one not worthy of serious refutation.

This imperfect effort to illustrate the nature and results of our land-revenue policy in Northern India, and to suggest some reforms in our mode of assessing and collecting the land-tax may here be fitly concluded, and no one can be more sensible of its shortcomings than the writer. No attempt has been made to palliate the faults of the landowners themselves, or to deny that in many cases their ruin is due solely to their own extravagance and mismanagement. It has been deemed sufficient to urge that the Government of this country is bound to reform its system of administration, if it can be established that that system in its operation is productive of serious evils and much individual hardship; an endeavour has been made to show that the embarrassments of the landowners can be frequently traced to over-taxation by the Government, to harshness in the collection of the revenue, and to the unsuitableness of our laws and of our procedure to the native character; and it is believed that some of the proposed remedies might be found both applicable and feasible.

If some such remedial measures are adopted, there may be reason to hope that in the future the landed proprietors of these provinces will be unable to trace the loss of their ancestral estates to over-taxation by the land-revenue-assessors, or to the relentlessness of our system of collection; no utopian schemes have been proposed, but simple and easy changes in our system of administration; the matters here detailed are ripe for decision, and it is time that the Government should at least awake to the pressing necessity of carrying into immediate operation some remedies either of the nature proposed or of any other practicable character, for the reform of our revenue administration is a question which demands and should secure prompt and careful settlement.

APPENDIX I.

Mouza *Amarsa.*—An imperfect pattidari village, held by a proprietary body of 23 Chauhans; all the cultivated land divided, save some 30 bighas of jungle land not yet brought under the plough; an average village, but there is one *har* on the west which is all hard matyar land without any wells or tanks, and cultivators only accept batai leases. The khewat shows that the proprietors are well-to-do, as there have been no sales or mortgages of shares; an analysis of the rent-roll shows as follows, *viz.* :—

I.—Zamindar's seer:

			Bighas.	Rent.	Rate.
or Goind	Goind	...	20	...	Entered at
Manjhar	Domati	...	35	...	Re. 1-8
Palo	Matyar	...	10	...	all round.
	Bhur	...	15	...	
	Total	...	80	120	

And further sub-divided, if desirable, into irrigated and unirrigated.

II.—High-caste cultivators:

			Bighas.	Rs.	As.	Rs.	As.
Goind	...	...	25	62	0	2	8
Domati	...	...	40	80	0	2	0
Matyar	...	...	5	10	0	2	0
Bhur	...	...	10	10	0	1	0
	Total	...	80	162	0		

III.—Low-caste cultivators:

			Bighas.	Rs.	As.	Rs.	As.
Goind	...	...	30	90	0	3	0
Matyar	...	...	15	37	8	2	8
Domati	...	..	45	112	8	2	8
Bhur	...	...	20	30	0	1	8
	Total	...	110	270	0		

IV.—Maafis, sankallaps, and khidmati lands:

	Bighas.	Rent.	Rate.
Goind	3	...	
Domati	6	...	
Matyar	4	...	
Bhur	10	...	
Total ...	23	Rent-free tenures.	

V.—Batai lands:

	Bighas.
Goind	*Nil*
Domati } at half and half	5
Matyar } at half and half	10
Bhur, at one-third of produce	20
Total ...	35

It will be seen that, as in other villages about this neighbourhood, the high-caste cultivators pay rents at favorable rates; the jamabandi has been regularly tested by the Kanungo; it shows rents of Rs. 3 for goind, Rs. 2 for domati, Rs. 2-8 for matyar, and Re. 1-8 for bhur in respect to the low-caste tenants-at-will; personal enquiry and a general comparison of the rent-rolls of these villages about Amarsa show that these are the rents actually paid, and there is not the slightest reason to doubt the correctness of the returns. In some villages the goind fetches Rs. 3-8, but here is no tobacco, or poppy cultivation.

Assessing the seer, which is only given as paying Re. 1-8 all round at full high-caste rates, the rent-roll is swelled by Rs. 42. Then there are the maafis, &c.; assuming high-caste rents for all the lands of this class the rental is increased by Rs. 37.

There remain the batai fields; these are very poor, and in many years they lie quite fallow; they might perhaps be assessed at rents of 8 annas a bigha all round; this gives an increase of Rs. 17 to the estimated assets.

Finally there is the untilled jungle-ground; it is not probable, however, that this will soon be cut, as the cattle graze there, and the wood is required for fuel; it is not good land, and the probability of its being broken up is not great. I would not assess it at all. The dhak leaves are wanted for the cane-boiling.

There is no land liable to floods, and the produce of all but the batai fields is tolerably certain.

The present jama is Rs. 150; the computed rental amounts to Rs. 720; this gives a jama of Rs. 360; or an increase of over Rs. 170.

To exact this sum at once would assuredly ruin these hitherto prosperous and punctual revenue-payers; I would increase it after one year by 20 per cent., and raise it by 20 per cent. every three years till it reaches Rs. 360, the proper demand at half assets.

Mr. Carnegy, in his Notes on Assessments (pp. 122-123), gives his objections to an assessment based on deductions from the rent-roll as follows; he regards it as unreliable:—

1. Because ex-proprietors hold lands at low rates, and therefore these lands are not represented at the rack-rental.

If however no consideration is to be shown to the present owner, it is easy to assess these at the full rates, which, as the rent-roll shows, are paid by other cultivators.

2. Cultivators pay very high rates for their arable land, under a direct understanding with the owner that they are to gather grass and wood from the village waste; if these high rents are taken and the waste is also assessed, that the owner is taxed twice over. As a rule, however, all resident tenants enjoy this privilege gratis, and it is very unusual for them to pay any rent for it; in the exceptional cases where they do thus pay, the high returned rents will show the assessor that an enquiry is necessary, and he can easily allow for this peculiar system of payment either by not assessing the waste at all, or by taxing it very leniently.

3. Many rent-rolls have been inordinately run up by reason of sub-proprietary disputes.

But the unusual rates will show the assessor that there is something wrong, and if the village is a sub-settled one, the under-proprietor, and not the superior owner, is responsible for the rent-roll; the latter has no power to write it up with a view to obtain the over-assessment of his sub-holder's estate.

If the estate is not a sub-settled one, the owner would lose more than he would gain by this practice; he would lose on all the khalsa land, and only gain by securing a high assessment for the few sub-holders' land, even should he succeed in deceiving the Kanungo and the settlement officer.

4. Many proprietors are in debt to their cultivators, and pay the interest in a reduction of rent.

But a slavish obedience to the rent-roll is nowhere enjoined; in this case the low level of the rates will show the assessor that there is something requiring investigation, and if he finds this low rent to be due to this cause, he can assess the village at the rents paid by the tenants of adjoining estates.

5. It was customary to make advances to new cultivators, and these advances were repaid by the addition of an anna or two per bigha, or per rupee; to assess this anna or two would be to tax capital.

But here the rents would be higher than the ordinary rent, and if on enquiry the assessor found this to be the case, he could make allowances in assuming the gross rental.

It is to be observed also, that in no single district, save in the isolated cases of European properties, has any regard been paid to the principle of not taxing capital; when assessors tax the village waste without scruple, and some even discount the possible rise in rents, an assessment, which only takes half the return for an advance to a cultivator, does comparatively little harm.

6. Lands were set aside for retainers and village servants, who held rent-free in lieu of wages.

But it is clear, that if only the area of this land is correctly ascertained, there is no difficulty whatever in assessing it at full rates.

The other objections do not require detailed notice.